Changing the Size of a Quilt Pattern

Adjusting the size of a quilt design to fit the bed that you want it to fit is not always easy to do. In this book, we give you eight quilts, each with a different setting, and instructions for adjusting the size of any quilt with that setting. We also give you complete instructions for making each quilt as well as information for making the quilts in five specific sizes: crib/throw, twin, double, queen and king.

The first step in adjusting the size of a quilt is to know what size you want to make the quilt. Begin by measuring the length and width of the mattress top or area you want to cover. Then decide on how much drop you want on the sides. Remember to double this measurement when adding this amount to the quilt size since the drop is the same for both sides and usually the same for the top and bottom.

Next, select the quilt design you want to make, either from this book or from another book. If it is from another book, look for the quilt setting in this book that best matches the quilt setting of your selected design. At the beginning of the instructions, you will find information for adjusting the quilt size for that quilt setting. Remember to adjust the amount of fabric needed for the borders when you add blocks or make changes to the quilt size.

We hope you enjoy stitching these bed quilts and discover new ways to adjust the size of your favorite quilt designs.

Here are the settings we used.

House of White Birches, Berne, Indiana 46711   Clotilde.com

Pathways

Design by Julie Weaver

Strip-pieced blocks are quick and easy to stitch. It's simple to add more or take away blocks to change the size of the quilt.

Adjusting the Quilt Size

When you want to change the size of a quilt that has blocks all the same size, you should first check the size of the block. In this case, the block size is 10" x 10", so increasing or decreasing the size means a difference of a multiple of 10. To make the quilt a size that is not a multiple of 10, you will need to change the size of the borders, remembering that for every inch you add to the border, you are adding two inches to the width and two inches to the length of the quilt. If you don't want to change the size of the current border(s), then you will need to add another border to obtain the size you want.

Project Specifications

Skill Level: Beginner
Quilt Size: 78" x 98"
Block Size: 10" x 10"
Number of Blocks: 35

Pathways
10" x 10" Block
Make 35

Materials

- 1 yard tan print
- 1¼ yards cream floral
- 2⅔ yards black small floral
- 3⅜ yards black large floral
- Batting 84" x 104"
- Backing 84" x 104"
- All-purpose thread to match fabrics

- Quilting thread
- Basic sewing tools and supplies

Cutting

1. Cut three 10½" by fabric width strips black large floral; subcut strips into (35) 3½" A rectangles.

2. Cut eight 10½" by fabric width G strips black large floral.   *Border*

3. Cut four 10½" by fabric width strips cream floral; subcut strips into (70) 2" B rectangles.

4. Cut three 10½" by fabric width strips each black small floral (C) and tan print (D); subcut strips into (70) 1½" rectangles each for C and D.

5. Cut (15) 2½" by fabric width E/F/H/I strips black small floral.

6. Cut nine 2¼" by fabric width strips black small floral for binding.

Completing the Blocks

Note: Use a ¼" seam allowance for all stitching. Sew all seams with right sides together.

1. To complete one Pathways block, sew B to each long side of A; press seams toward B.

2. Add C to each B side of the A-B unit and then add D in the same manner to complete one block; press seams toward C and then D.

3. Repeat steps 1 and 2 to complete 35 Pathways blocks.

Finishing the Top

1. Join five Pathways blocks to make an X row, turning every other block referring to Figure 1; press seams in one direction. Repeat to make four X rows.

X Row
Make 4

Figure 1

2. Join five Pathways blocks to make a Y row, turning every other block referring to Figure 2; press seams in one direction. Repeat to make three Y rows.

Y Row
Make 3

Figure 2

3. Arrange and join the rows, alternating X and Y rows and keeping seams in adjacent rows in opposite directions; press seams in one direction to complete the pieced center.

4. Join the E/F/H/I strips on short ends to make one long strip; press seams open. Subcut strip into two each 70½" E, 54½" F, 94½" H and 78½" I border strips.

5. Sew the E strips to opposite sides and F strips to the top and bottom of the pieced center; press seams toward E and F strips.

6. Join the G strips on short ends to make one long strip; press seams open. Subcut strip into four 74½" G border strips.

7. Sew a G strip to opposite sides and then to the top and bottom of the pieced center; press seams toward G strips.

8. Sew an H strip to opposite long sides and I strips to the top and bottom of the pieced center to complete the top; press seams toward H and I strips.

Finishing the Quilt

1. Sandwich batting between the completed top and prepared backing piece; pin or baste layers together to hold flat.

2. Quilt as desired by hand or machine; remove pins or basting. Trim batting and backing even with the top.

3. Join the binding strips with right sides together on short ends to make one long strip; press seams open.

4. Press the strip in half with wrong sides together along length.

5. Sew the binding to the right side of the quilt edges, mitering corners and overlapping ends.

6. Fold binding to the back side and stitch in place. ❖

Tip

If you prefer to strip-piece the blocks, simply stitch fabric width strips together in the same order as the pieces, pressing seams of the strips in the same manner as directed in instructions. Subcut strip sets sections into four 10½" blocks each to complete the blocks as shown in Figure 3. Be careful not to stretch the strips as you stitch. This will make the stitched strip sets a bit wavy and make it harder to have accurate blocks.

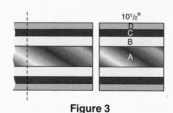

Figure 3

Twin-Size Pathways
Placement Diagram 78" x 98"

Crib-Size Pathways
Placement Diagram 46" x 46"

Crib-Size Pathways

46" x 46"
9 Pathways blocks–10" x 10"
9 A strips (1 strip)
18 B strips (1 strip)
18 C strips (1 strip)
18 D strips (1 strip)
8 E/F/H/I strips (30½" E, 34½" F, 42½" H, 46½" I)
4 G strips (4½" wide) (34½", 42½")
5 binding strips

Materials
- ⅜ yard tan print
- ⅜ yard cream floral
- 1 yard black large floral
- 1⅓ yards black small floral
- Batting 52" x 52"
- Backing 52" x 52"

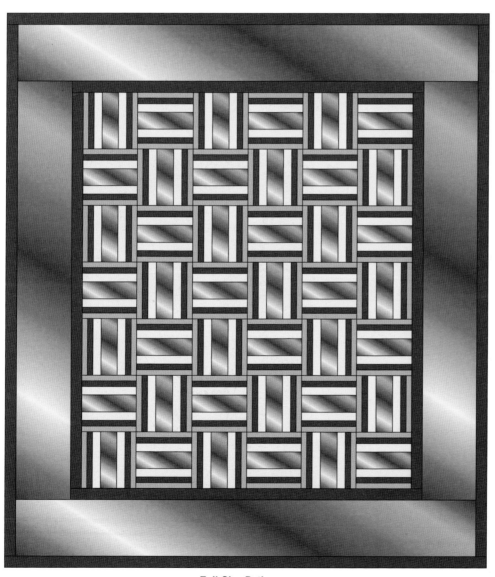

Full-Size Pathways
Placement Diagram 88" x 98"

Full-Size Pathways

88" x 98"
42 Pathways blocks
 –10" x 10"
42 A strips (4 strips)
84 B strips (4 strips)
84 C strips (3 strips)
84 D strips (3 strips)
16 E/F/H/I strips (70½" E,
 64½" F, 94½" H, 88½" I)
8 G strips (74½", 84½")
10 binding strips

Materials
- 1 yard tan print
- 1⅓ yards cream floral
- 2⅞ yards black
 small floral
- 3⅔ black large floral
- Batting 94" x 104"
- Backing 94" x 104"

House of White Birches, Berne, Indiana 46711 Clotilde.com

6

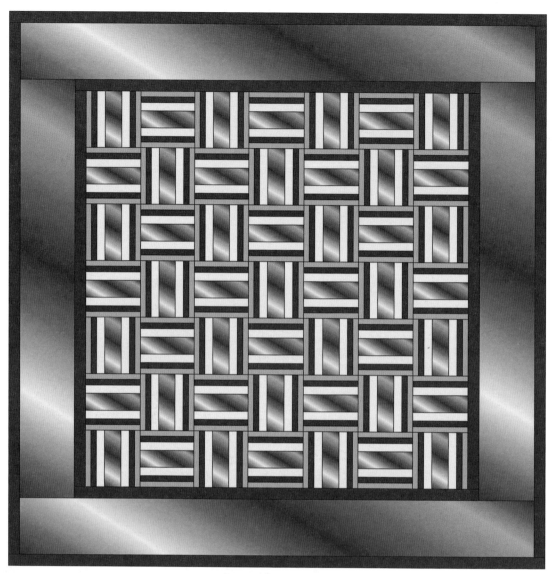

Queen-Size Pathways
Placement Diagram 98" x 98"

Queen-Size Pathways

98" x 98"
49 Pathways blocks–10" x 10"
49 A strips (5 strips)
98 B strips (5 strips)
98 C strips (4 strips)
98 D strips (4 strips)
17 E/F/H/I strips (70½" E, 74½" F,
  94½" H, 98½" I)
9 G strips (74½", 94½")
10 binding strips

Materials

B • 1¼ yards tan print *lite green*
D • 1⅝ yards cream floral *green*
C • 3¼ yards black small floral
A • 4¼ yards black large floral – *focal*
• Batting 104" x 104"
• Backing 104" x 104"

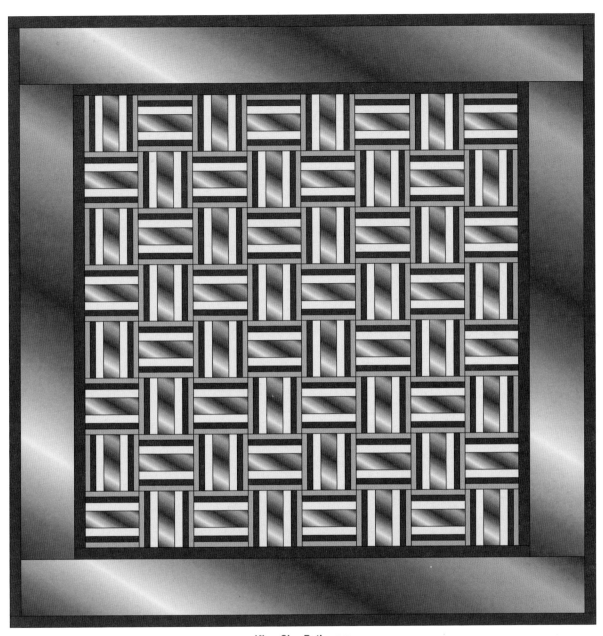

King-Size Pathways
Placement Diagram 108" x 108"

King-Size Pathways
108" x 108"
64 Pathways blocks–10" x 10"
64 A strips (6 strips)
128 B strips (7 strips)
128 C strips (5 strips)
128 D strips (5 strips)
18 E/F/H/I strips (80½" E, 84½" F,
    104½" H, 108½" I)
10 G strips (84½", 104½")
11 binding strips

Materials
• 1⅝ yards tan print
• 2¼ yards cream floral
• 3⅝ yards black small floral
• 4⅞ yards black large floral
• Batting 114" x 114"
• Backing 114" x 114"

House of White Birches, Berne, Indiana 46711   Clotilde.com

Season of Change

Design by Julie Weaver

A variety of autumn tonals stand out on a light background in the leaf blocks of this pretty quilt.

Adjusting the Quilt Size

This quilt setting is a slight variation of the Pathways quilt. The blocks are all the same size, in this case 9" x 9", but the designer has added sashing between the columns. Instead of increasing or decreasing by the size of the block, you will need to use a multiple of the block size and the sashing size. Adding sashing between the columns is one way of increasing the width of a quilt without increasing the length. This technique can be used with many quilt designs, giving your quilt a whole new look.

Project Specifications

Skill Level: Beginner
Quilt Size: 56" x 59"
Block Size: 9" x 9"
Number of Blocks: 20

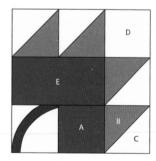

Maple Leaf
9" x 9" Block
Make 20

Materials

- 20 (5" x 18") rectangles assorted cream/tan/white scraps
- 20 (5" x 12") assorted fall-colored scraps
- 20 (5" x 10") assorted fall-colored scraps
- 20 (2" x 6") stem-colored scraps
- ½ yard cream tonal
- 2 yards brown mottled
- Backing 62" x 65"
- Batting 62" x 65"
- ½ yard fusible web
- ½ yard fabric stabilizer

- All-purpose thread to match fabrics
- Quilting thread
- ½ yard 18"-wide fusible web
- ½ yard fabric stabilizer
- Basic sewing tools and supplies

Cutting

1. Cut two 3½" x 3½" D squares each cream/tan/white scrap.

2. Cut two 3⅞" x 3⅞" C squares each cream/tan/white scrap.

3. Cut one 3½" x 6½" E rectangle each 5" x 12" fall-colored scrap.

4. Cut one 3½" x 3½" A square each 5" x 12" fall-colored scrap.

5. Cut two 3⅞" x 3⅞" B squares each 5" x 10" fall-colored scrap.

6. Prepare stem template using pattern given; trace onto the paper side of the fusible web as directed on pattern. Cut out shapes, leaving a margin around each one; fuse shapes to the stem-colored scraps. Cut out shapes on traced lines; remove paper backing.

7. Cut four 1" by fabric width F strips cream tonal.

8. Cut five 1½" by fabric width J/K strips cream tonal.

9. Cut seven 1¼" by fabric width G strips brown mottled.

10. Cut five 2½" by fabric width H/I strips brown mottled.

11. Cut six 4½" by fabric width L/M strips brown mottled.

12. Cut six 2¼" by fabric width strips brown mottled for binding.

13. Cut (20) 3½" x 3½" squares fabric stabilizer.

Completing the Blocks

1. Cut (20) 3" x 3" squares fabric stabilizer.
Note: Use a ¼" seam allowance for all stitching. Sew all seams with right sides together.

2. Draw a diagonal line from corner to corner on the wrong side of each C square.

3. To complete one Maple Leaf block, select two matching each B, C and D squares, and one each matching A square and E rectangle.

4. Place one C square on one B square with right sides together; stitch ¼" on each side of the marked line as shown in Figure 1; cut apart on the marked line and press seam toward B to complete two B-C units, again referring to Figure 1. Repeat with the second B and C squares to complete a total of four B-C units.

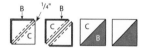

Figure 1

5. Arrange and fuse a stem piece to one D square as shown in Figure 2. Pin a square of fabric stabilizer to the wrong side of the fused square.

Figure 2

6. Using thread to match the stem fabric and a machine buttonhole stitch, stitch along the curved edges of the stem to hold in place. Remove fabric stabilizer.

7. Join the E rectangle with one B-C unit to complete the center row as shown in Figure 3; press seams in one direction.

Figure 3

8. Join one B-C unit, the A square and the stem unit to make the bottom row as shown in Figure 4; press seams in the opposite direction from the center row.

Figure 4

9. Join two B-C units with D to make the top row as shown in Figure 5; press seams in opposite direction from the center row.

Figure 5

10. Join the rows referring to the block drawing for positioning; press seams in one direction.

11. Repeat Steps 3–10 to complete 20 Maple Leaf blocks.

Completing the Top

1. Join five Maple Leaf blocks to make a vertical X row as shown in Figure 6; press seams in one direction. Repeat to make two vertical rows.

X Row
Make 2

Y Row
Make 2

Figure 6

2. Join five Maple Leaf blocks to make a vertical Y row, again referring to Figure 6; press seams in one direction. Repeat to make two vertical Y rows.

3. Join the F strips on short ends to make one long strip; press seams open. Subcut strip into three 45½" F strips.

4. Join the G strips on short ends to make one long strip; press seams open; subcut strip into six 45½" G strips.

5. Sew an F strip with right sides together between two G strips to make an F-G strip set as shown in Figure 7; press seams toward G strips.

F   G

Figure 7

6. Join the vertical rows with the F-G strip sets referring to the Placement Diagram for positioning of strips; press seams toward the F-G strip sets.

7. Join the H/I strips on short ends to make one long strip; press seams open. Subcut strip into two 45½" H strips and two 46½" I strips.

8. Sew an H strip to opposite long sides and I strips to the top and bottom of the pieced center; press seams toward the H and I strips.

9. Join the J/K strips on short ends to make one long strip; press seams open. Subcut strip into two 49½" J strips and two 48½" K strips.

10. Sew a J strip to opposite long sides and K strips to the top and bottom of the pieced center; press seams toward the J and K strips.

11. Join the L/M strips on short ends to make one long strip; press seams open. Subcut strip into two 51½" L strips and two 56½" M strips.

12. Sew an L strip to opposite long sides and M strips to the top and bottom of the pieced center to complete the pieced top; press seams toward the L and M strips.

Finishing the Quilt

1. Sandwich batting between the completed top and prepared backing piece; pin or baste layers together to hold flat.

2. Quilt as desired by hand or machine; remove pins or basting. Trim batting and backing even with the top.

3. Join the binding strips with right sides together on short ends to make one long strip; press seams open.

4. Press the strip in half with wrong sides together along length.

5. Sew the binding to the right side of the quilt edges, mitering corners and overlapping ends.

6. Fold binding to the back side and stitch in place. ❖

Twin-Size Season of Change
Placement Diagram 67" x 86"

Lap-Size Season of Change
Placement Diagram 56" x 59"

Twin-Size Season of Change
67" x 86"
40 Maple Leaf blocks–9" x 9"
40 A squares
80 each B, C and D squares
40 E rectangles
7 F strips (72½")
14 G strips (72½")
7 H/I strips (72½" H, 57½" I)
7 J/K strips (76½" J, 59½" K)
7 L/M strips (78½" L, 67½" M)
40 stems
8 binding strips

Materials
- 40 (5" x 18") rectangles assorted cream/tan/white scraps
- 40 (5" x 12") assorted fall-colored scraps
- 40 (5" x 10") assorted fall-colored scraps
- 40 (2" x 6") stem-colored scraps
- ⅝ yard cream tonal
- 2⅝ yards brown mottled
- Backing 73" x 92"
- Batting 73" x 92"
- ¾ yard 18"-wide fusible web
- 1 yard fabric stabilizer

12

Full-Size Season of Change
Placement Diagram 78" x 86"

Full-Size Season of Change
78" x 86"
48 Maple Leaf blocks–9" x 9"
48 A squares
96 each B, C and D squares
48 E rectangles
9 F strips (72½")
18 G strips (72½")
7 H/I strips (72½" H, 68½" I)
7 J/K strips (76½" J, 70½" K)
8 L/M strips (78½" L, 78½" M)
48 stems
9 binding strips

Materials
- 48 (5" x 18") rectangles assorted cream/tan/white scraps
- 48 (5" x 12") assorted fall-colored scraps
- 48 (5" x 10") assorted fall-colored scraps
- 48 (2" x 6") stem-colored scraps
- ⅔ yard cream tonal
- 2⅞ yards brown mottled
- Backing 84" x 92"
- Batting 84" x 92"
- ¾ yard 18"-wide fusible web
- 1¼ yards fabric stabilizer

Queen-Size Season of Change
Placement Diagram 89" x 95"

Queen-Size Season of Change
89" x 95"
63 Maple Leaf blocks–9" x 9"
63 A squares
126 each B, C and D squares
63 E rectangles
12 F strips (81½")
24 G strips (81½")
8 H/I strips (81½" H, 79½" I)
8 J/K strips (85½" J, 81½" K)
9 L/M strips (87½" L, 89½" M)
63 stems
10 binding strips

Materials
- 63 (5" x 18") rectangles assorted cream/tan/white scraps
- 63 (5" x 12") assorted fall-colored scraps
- 63 (5" x 10") assorted fall-colored scraps
- 63 (2" x 6") stem-colored scraps
- ¾ yard cream tonal
- 3⅓ yards brown mottled
- Backing 95" x 101"
- Batting 95" x 101"
- 1 yard 18"-wide fusible web
- 1½ yards fabric stabilizer

King-Size Season of Change
Placement Diagram 100" x 113"

King-Size Season of Change

100" x 113"
88 Maple Leaf blocks–9" x 9"
88 A squares
176 each B, C and D squares
88 E rectangles
17 F strips (99½")
34 G strips (99½")
10 H/I strips (99½" H, 90½" I)
10 J/K strips (103½" J, 92½" K)
10 L/M strips (105½" L, 100½" M)
88 stems
11 binding strips

Materials

- 88 (5" x 18") rectangles assorted cream/tan/white scraps
- 88 (5" x 12") assorted fall-colored scraps
- 88 (5" x 10") assorted fall-colored scraps
- 88 (2" x 6") stem-colored scraps
- 1 yard cream tonal
- 4⅛ yards brown mottled
- Backing 106" x 119"
- Batting 106" x 119"
- 1⅓ yards 18"-wide fusible web
- 2 yards fabric stabilizer

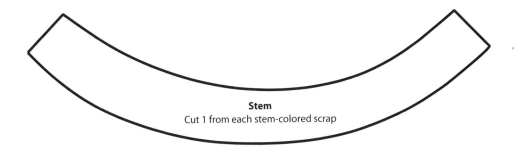

Stem
Cut 1 from each stem-colored scrap

Tip

You may buy yardage of fall-colored fabrics and make a planned quilt using the resulting blocks.

This lap-size quilt would make a beautiful wall quilt to hang in a prominent place in your home.

House of White Birches, Berne, Indiana 46711   Clotilde.com

Climbing Jacob's Ladder

Design by Constance Ewbank

One simple block in black and white with red accents creates a striking quilt.

Adjusting the Quilt Size

Although this setting looks like the blocks are placed on the diagonal, a closer look reveals that it is the typical setting of blocks in rows and columns. To change the size of the quilt, it is easiest to add or delete a row or column of blocks. To make further adjustments, you will need to change the size of the borders or add more borders.

Project Specifications

- Skill Level: Beginner
- Quilt Size: 70" x 91"
- Block Size: 10½" x 10½"
- Number of Blocks: 48

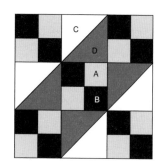

Jacob's Ladder
10½" x 10½" Block
Make 48

Materials

- 1⅓ yards white tonal
- 2⅛ yards total black-with-white prints
- 2⅛ yards total white-with-black prints
- 2⅞ yards red mottled
- Batting 76" x 97"
- Backing 76" x 97"
- All-purpose thread to match fabrics
- Quilting thread
- Basic sewing tools and supplies

Cutting

1. Cut (27) 2¼" by fabric width strips each white-with-black (A) and black-with-white (B) prints.

2. Cut (11) 4⅜" by fabric width strips each white tonal (C) and red mottled (D). Subcut strips into (96) 4⅜" C and D squares. Cut each C and D square in half on one diagonal to make 192 each C and D triangles.

3. Cut eight 4" by fabric width E/F strips red mottled.

4. Cut eight 2¼" by fabric width strips red mottled for binding.

Completing the Blocks

Note: *Use a ¼" seam allowance for all stitching. Sew all seams with right sides together.*

1. Sew an A strip to a B strip with right sides together along length; press seam toward B strips. Repeat to make 27 strip sets.

2. Subcut A-B strip sets into a total of 480 (2¼") A-B units as shown in Figure 1.

Figure 1

3. Stack same-fabric A-B units together in piles.

4. Sew C to D along the diagonals to make a C-D unit; press seam toward D. Repeat to make 192 C-D units.

5. To complete one Jacob's Ladder block, select 10 same-fabric A-B units; join two A-B units to make a Four-Patch unit as shown in Figure 2; press seam in one direction. Repeat to make five Four-Patch units.

Figure 2

6. Sew a C-D unit between two Four-Patch units to make a top row as shown in Figure 3; press seams toward Four-Patch units. Repeat to make the bottom row.

Figure 3

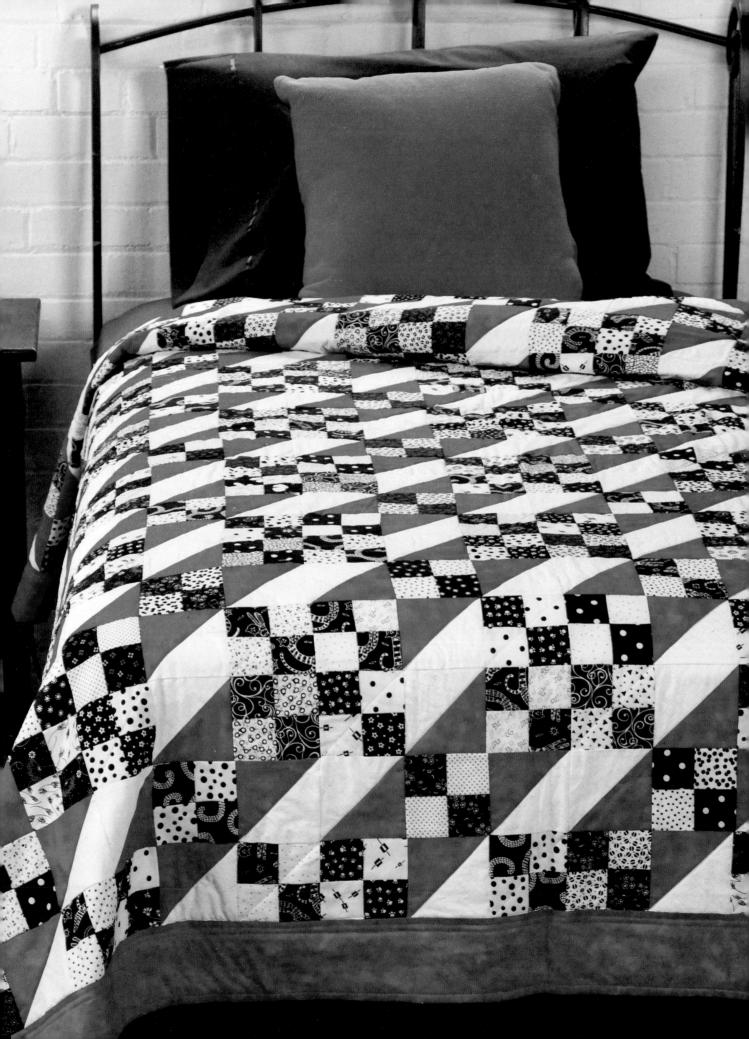

7. Sew a Four-Patch unit between two C-D units to make the center row as shown in Figure 4; press seams toward the Four-Patch unit.

Figure 4

8. Join the rows referring to the block drawing to complete one Jacob's Ladder block; press seams in one direction.

9. Repeat steps 5–8 to complete 48 Jacob's Ladder blocks.

Finishing the Top

1. Join six Jacob's Ladder blocks to make a row as shown in Figure 5; press seams in one direction. Repeat to make eight rows.

Figure 5

2. Join the rows with seams in adjoining rows in opposite directions; press seams in one direction.

3. Join the E-F strips on short ends to make one long strip; press seams open. Subcut strip into two 84½" E strips and two 70½" F strips.

4. Sew the E strips to opposite long sides and F strips to the top and bottom of the pieced center to complete the pieced top.

Finishing the Quilt

1. Sandwich batting between the completed top and prepared backing piece; pin or baste layers together to hold flat.

2. Quilt as desired by hand or machine; remove pins or basting. Trim batting and backing even with the top.

3. Join the binding strips with right sides together on short ends to make one long strip; press seams open.

4. Press the strip in half with wrong sides together along length.

5. Sew the binding to the right side of the quilt edges, mitering corners and overlapping ends.

6. Fold binding to the back side and stitch in place. ❖

Twin-Size Climbing Jacob's Ladder
Placement Diagram 70" x 91"

Tip

The Jacob's Ladder blocks may be arranged in several different ways to create different designs. Try a couple of different arrangements before sewing your blocks together in rows. You may prefer to join the blocks in a totally different arrangement than the one shown.

Crib-Size Climbing Jacob's Ladder
Placement Diagram 38½" x 49"

Crib-Size Climbing Jacob's Ladder

38½" x 49"
12 Jacob's Ladder blocks–10½" x 10½"
120 A-B units (7 strips each)
24 C squares (3 strips to make 48 C triangles)
24 D squares (3 strips to make 48 D triangles)
4 E/F strips (42½" E, 39" F)
5 binding strips

Materials

- ½ yard white tonal
- ⅝ yard total black-with-white prints
- ⅝ yard total white-with-black prints
- 1⅓ yards red mottled
- Batting 45" x 55"
- Backing 45" x 55"

Full-Size Climbing Jacob's Ladder
Placement Diagram 80½" x 91"

Full-Size Climbing Jacob's Ladder

80½" x 91"
56 Jacob's Ladder blocks–10½" x 10½"
560 A-B units (32 strips each)
112 C squares (13 strips to make 224 C triangles)
112 D squares (13 strips to make 224 D triangles)
8 E-F strips (84½" E, 81" F)
9 binding strips

Materials

- 1¾ yards white tonal
- 2⅜ yards total black-with-white prints
- 2⅜ yards total white-with-black prints
- 3¼ yards red mottled
- Batting 87" x 97"
- Backing 87" x 97"

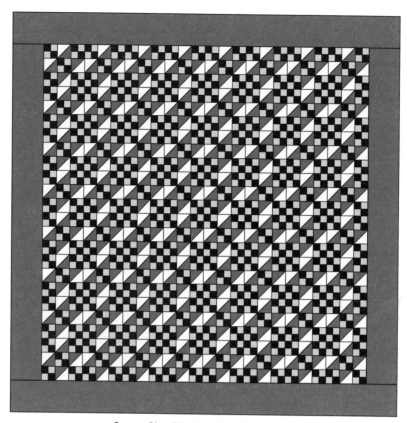

Queen-Size Climbing Jacob's Ladder
Placement Diagram 100" x 100"

Queen-Size Climbing Jacob's Ladder
100" x 100"
64 Jacob's Ladder blocks–10½" x 10½"
640 A-B units (36 strips each)
128 C squares (15 strips to make 256 C triangles)
128 D squares (15 strips to make 256 D triangles)
9 E/F strips (cut 8½" wide) (84½" E, 100½" F)
10 binding strips

Materials
• 2 yards white tonal
• 2⅜ yards total black-with-white prints
• 2⅜ yards total white-with-black prints
• 4¾ yards red mottled
• Batting 106" x 106"
• Backing 106" x 106"

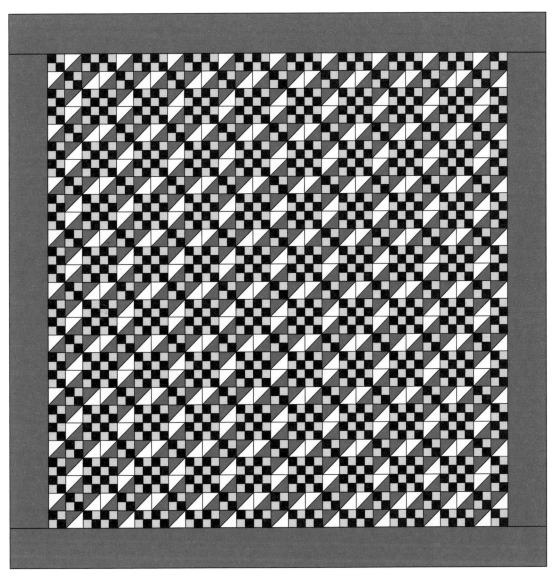

King-Size Climbing Jacob's Ladder
Placement Diagram 110½" x 110½"

King-Size Climbing Jacob's Ladder
110½" x 110½"
81 Jacob's Ladder blocks–10½" x 10½"
810 A-B units (45 strips each)
162 C squares (18 strips to make 324 C triangles)
162 D squares (18 strips to make 324 D triangles)
10 E/F strips (8½" wide) (95" E, 111" F)
11 binding strips

Materials
- 2⅓ yards white tonal
- 3 yards total black-with-white prints
- 3 yards total white-with-black prints
- 5½ yards red mottled
- Batting 118" x 118"
- Backing 118" x 118"

Dragonfly Dreams

Design by Lucy A. Fazely & Michael L. Burns

Summertime brings the dragonflies out to bask in the warmth of the sun. Stay warm yourself under this pretty quilt.

Adjusting the Quilt Size

When two quilt blocks are used, you adjust the quilt size the same as for a typical quilt, by adding or deleting rows or columns of blocks. This quilt very creatively uses half blocks at the beginning and end of some of the rows. Even so, it is easiest to adjust this quilt by 9"-block increments. The adventure-some quilter can adjust the size by half a pieced block if he/she places the half blocks randomly on each row, matching the random placement of the appliqués on the border. Other options are increasing or decreasing the size of the border or adding multiple borders.

Project Specifications

Skill Level: Beginner
Quilt Size: 72" x 81"
Block Size: 9" x 9"
Number of Blocks: 42

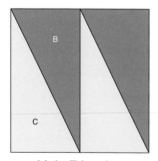

Light Triangles
9" x 9" Block
Make 20

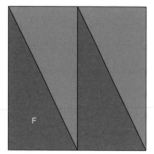

Dark Triangles
9" x 9" Block
Make 4

Dragonfly
9" x 9" Block
Make 18

Materials

- ¼ yard purple tonal
- ⅜ yard light pink tonal
- 1⅛ yards dark pink tonal
- 1¼ yards medium green tonal
- 2 yards dark green print
- 2½ yards light green tonal
- Backing 78" x 87"
- Batting 78" x 87"
- All-purpose thread to match fabrics
- Quilting thread
- Clear nylon monofilament
- 3 yards 12"-wide fusible web
- 5½ yards 20"-wide fabric stabilizer
- Basting spray
- Basic sewing tools and supplies

Cutting

1. Cut eight 2¼" by fabric width strips dark pink tonal for binding.

2. Prepare a template for B/C/F pieces using pattern given.

3. Cut four 9½" by fabric width strips medium green tonal; subcut strips into 56 B pieces using template and referring to Figure 1.

Figure 1

4. Cut one 9½" by fabric width strip dark green print; subcut strip into eight F pieces using template.

5. Cut six 9½" by fabric width D/E strips dark green print.

6. Cut four 9½" by fabric width strips light green tonal; subcut strips into 48 C pieces using template.

7. Cut five 9½" by fabric width strips light green tonal; subcut strips into (18) 9½" A squares.

Tip

When changing the size of a quilt that includes both appliquéd and pieced blocks combined with randomly placed appliqué motifs, you have a lot of freedom to arrange blocks and appliqué motifs in various ways. Although the sample drawings shown stick to the original layout in many ways, you may vary your placement as you wish to create a unique quilt all your own using the sizes and number of blocks given.

Completing the Dragonfly Blocks

Note: *Use a ¼" seam allowance for all stitching. Sew all seams with right sides together.*

1. Trace appliqué shapes given onto the paper side of the fusible web as directed on each piece for number to cut; cut out shapes, leaving a margin around each one.

2. Fuse the shapes to the wrong side of the fabrics as directed on each piece for color. Cut out shapes on traced lines; remove paper backing.

3. Arrange and fuse one dragonfly motif in numerical order on each A square referring to the block drawing for positioning.

4. Cut fabric stabilizer into (30) 10" squares. Spray-baste a square of stabilizer to the wrong side of each A square.

5. Machine satin-stitch around each appliqué shape using clear nylon monofilament in the top of the machine and all-purpose thread to match A in the bobbin; remove fabric stabilizer when stitching is complete to complete the blocks.

6. Set aside remaining dragonfly pieces and stabilizer squares for borders.

Completing the Triangles Blocks

1. Sew B to C as shown in Figure 2; press seam toward B. Repeat to make 48 B-C units. Set aside eight units.

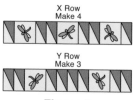

Figure 2

2. Join two B-C units to complete a Light Triangles block as shown in Figure 3; press seam in one direction. Repeat to make 20 blocks.

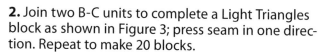

Figure 3

3. Sew B to F to complete a B-F unit as shown in Figure 4; press seams toward F. Repeat to make eight B-F units.

Figure 4

4. Join two B-F units to complete a Dark Triangles block referring to Figure 5; press seam in one direction. Repeat to make four blocks.

Figure 5

Completing the Top

1. Join three Dragonfly blocks with two Light Triangles blocks and two B-C units to make an X row referring to Figure 6; press seams toward the Dragonfly blocks. Repeat to make four X rows.

X Row
Make 4

Y Row
Make 3

Figure 6

2. Join four Light Triangles blocks with two Dragonfly blocks to make a Y row, again referring to Figure 6; press seams toward the Dragonfly blocks. Repeat to make three Y rows.

3. Join the X and Y rows referring to the Placement Diagram to complete the pieced center; press seams in one direction.

4. Join the D/E strips on short ends to make one long strip; press seams open. Subcut strip into two 63½" D strips and two 54½" E strips.

5. Sew a D strip to opposite long sides of the pieced center; press seams toward D strips.

6. Sew a Dark Triangles block to each end of each E strip as shown in Figure 7; press seams toward E strips.

Figure 7

7. Sew the E/block strips to the top and bottom of the pieced center; press seams toward the E/block strips.

8. Arrange and fuse dragonfly motifs on borders referring to the Placement Diagram for positioning.

9. Spray-baste a stabilizer square behind each motif and stitch in place as for blocks to complete the top.

Finishing the Quilt

1. Sandwich batting between the completed top and prepared backing piece; pin or baste layers together to hold flat.

2. Quilt as desired by hand or machine; remove pins or basting. Trim batting and backing even with the top.

3. Join the binding strips with right sides together on short ends to make one long strip; press seams open.

4. Press the strip in half with wrong sides together along length.

5. Sew the binding to the right side of the quilt edges, mitering corners and overlapping ends.

6. Fold binding to the back side and stitch in place. ❖

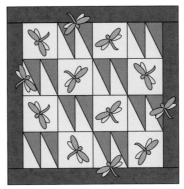

Crib-Size Dragonfly Dreams
Placement Diagram 44" x 44"

Crib-Size Dragonfly Dreams

44" x 44"
8 Dragonfly Blocks–9" x 9"
0 Dark Triangles Blocks–9" x 9"
8 Light Triangles Blocks–9" x 9"
8 A squares (2 strips)
16 B pieces (2 strips)
16 C pieces (2 strips)
4 D/E strips (4½" wide) (36½" D, 44½" E)
0 F pieces
Prepare 12 dragonfly motifs
5 binding strips

Materials
- ¼ yard purple tonal
- ¼ yard light pink tonal
- ⅝ yard dark green print
- ⅔ yard medium green tonal
- ¾ yard dark pink tonal
- 1¼ yards light green tonal
- Batting 50" x 50"
- Backing 50" x 50"
- 1¾ yards 12"-wide fusible web
- 2⅓ yards 20"-wide fabric stabilizer

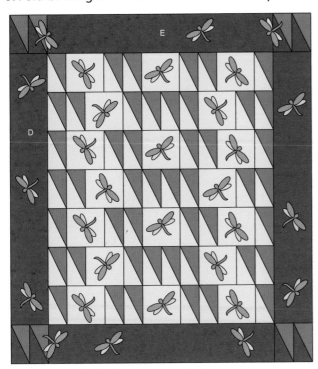

Twin-Size Dragonfly Dreams
Placement Diagram 72" x 81"

Full-Size Dragonfly Dreams

81" x 99"
32 Dragonfly blocks–9" x 9"
4 Dark Triangles blocks–9" x 9"
31 Light Triangles blocks–9" x 9"
32 A squares (8 strips)
70 B pieces (5 strips)
62 C pieces (5 strips)
7 D/E strips (81½" D, 63½" E)
8 F pieces (1 strip)
Prepare 48 dragonfly motifs
9 binding strips

Materials
- ⅜ yard purple tonal
- ½ yard light pink tonal
- 1¼ yards dark pink tonal
- 1½ yards medium green tonal
- 2¼ yards dark green print
- 3⅝ yards light green tonal
- Batting 86" x 105"
- Backing 86" x 105"
- 5½ yards 12"-wide fusible web
- 7¼ yards 20"-wide fabric stabilizer

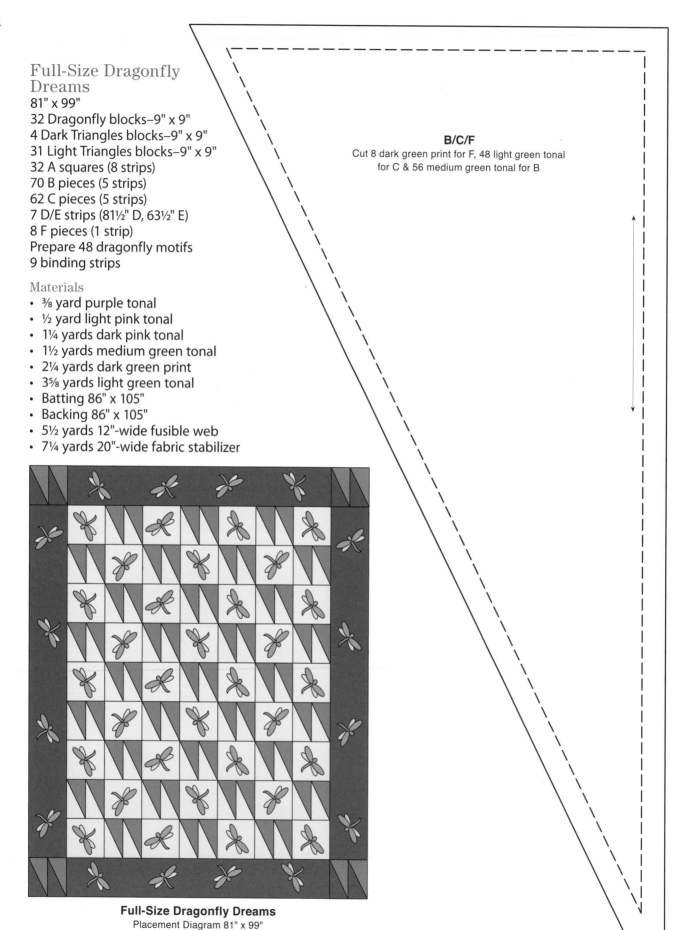

B/C/F
Cut 8 dark green print for F, 48 light green tonal
for C & 56 medium green tonal for B

Full-Size Dragonfly Dreams
Placement Diagram 81" x 99"

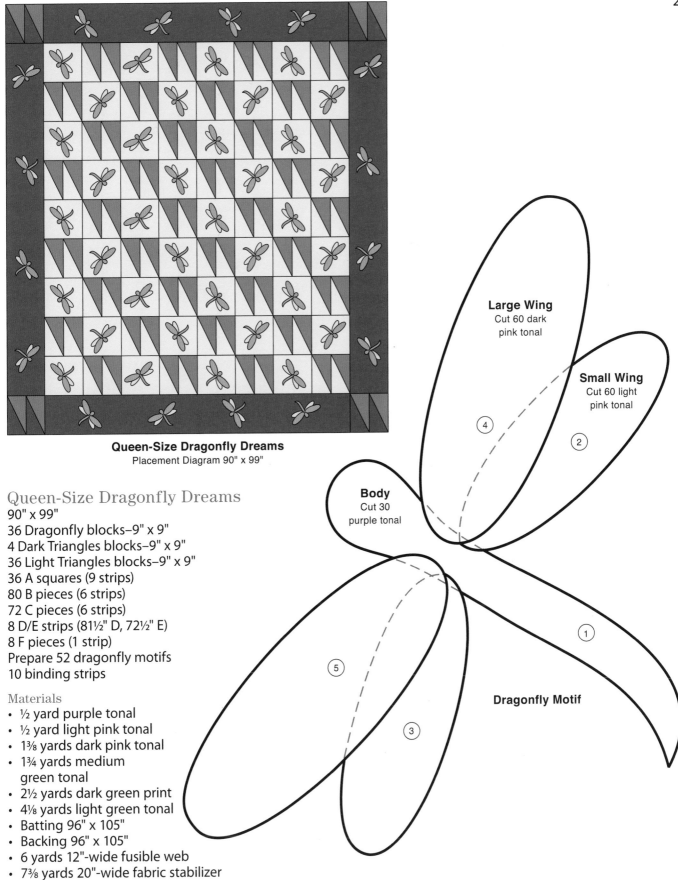

Queen-Size Dragonfly Dreams
Placement Diagram 90" x 99"

Queen-Size Dragonfly Dreams

90" x 99"
36 Dragonfly blocks–9" x 9"
4 Dark Triangles blocks–9" x 9"
36 Light Triangles blocks–9" x 9"
36 A squares (9 strips)
80 B pieces (6 strips)
72 C pieces (6 strips)
8 D/E strips (81½" D, 72½" E)
8 F pieces (1 strip)
Prepare 52 dragonfly motifs
10 binding strips

Materials
• ½ yard purple tonal
• ½ yard light pink tonal
• 1⅜ yards dark pink tonal
• 1¾ yards medium
  green tonal
• 2½ yards dark green print
• 4⅛ yards light green tonal
• Batting 96" x 105"
• Backing 96" x 105"
• 6 yards 12"-wide fusible web
• 7⅜ yards 20"-wide fabric stabilizer

Large Wing
Cut 60 dark
pink tonal

Small Wing
Cut 60 light
pink tonal

Body
Cut 30
purple tonal

Dragonfly Motif

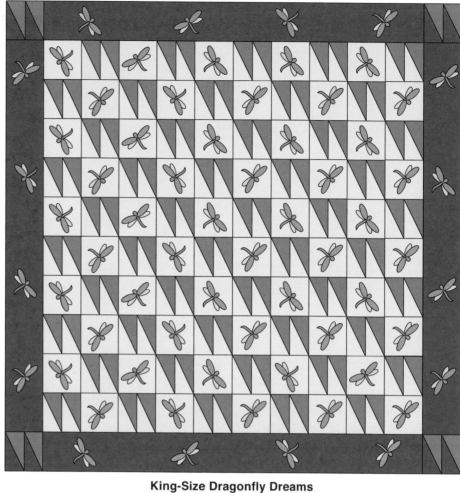

King-Size Dragonfly Dreams
Placement Diagram 108" x 108"

King-Size Dragonfly Dreams
108" x 108"
50 Dragonfly blocks–9" x 9"
4 Dark Triangles blocks–9" x 9"
50 Light Triangles blocks–9" x 9"
50 A squares (13 strips)
108 B pieces (8 strips)
100 C pieces (8 strips)
9 D/E strips (90½" D, 90½" E)
8 F pieces (1 strip)
Prepare 66 dragonfly motifs
11 binding strips

Materials
- ½ yard purple tonal
- ⅝ yard light pink tonal
- 1⅝ yards dark pink tonal
- 2¼ yards medium green tonal
- 2¾ yards dark green print
- 5⅔ yards light green tonal
- Batting 114" x 114"
- Backing 114" x 114"
- 7½ yards 12"-wide fusible web
- 9½ yards 20"-wide fabric stabilizer

Yo-Yo Garden Quilt

Design by Chris Malone

Use yo-yos to create a garden of flowers.

Adjusting the Quilt Size

Adding sashing is a good way to increase the size of a quilt. It also adds the option of changing the width of the sashing strips to increase or decrease the quilt size. If you decide to change the size by increasing or decreasing the number of blocks, remember that you need to use the size of the block plus the sashing width. In this quilt, the finished Flower block is a 10" square, and the finished sashing strips are 2" wide, so adding a row or a column means you are adding 12" to the width or length of the quilt.

Project Specifications

- Skill Level: Intermediate
- Quilt Size: 62" x 86"
- Block Size: 10" x 10", 6" x 6"
- Number of Blocks: 24, 4

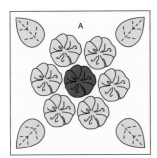

Flower
10" x 10" Block
Make 24

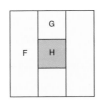

Corner
6" x 6" Block
Make 4

Materials

- ⅞ yard dark rose tonal
- 1 yard green mini-floral
- 1⅔ yards green/rose floral
- 3¼ yards cream mini-floral
- 3⅓ yards multicolored floral
- 1 yard thin fleece
- Batting 68" x 92"
- Backing 68" x 92"
- All-purpose thread to match fabrics
- Quilting thread
- Fabric glue stick (optional)
- Air/water soluble pen
- 28 (¾") buttons to cover
- Basic sewing tools and supplies

Cutting

1. Cut (10) 10½" by fabric width strips cream mini-floral; subcut strips into (24) 10½" A squares and (20) 6½" D rectangles.

2. Cut one 6½" by fabric width strip cream mini-floral; subcut strip into eight 2½" F strips and eight 2½" x 2½" G squares.

3. Cut four 10½" by fabric width strips green/rose floral; subcut strips into (58) 2½" B sashing strips.

4. Cut two 6½" by fabric width strips green/rose floral; subcut strips into (24) 2½" E strips.

5. Cut three 2½" by fabric width strips dark rose tonal; subcut strips into (35) 2½" C squares.

6. Prepare template for yo-yo using pattern given. Cut three 5¼" by fabric width strips dark rose tonal; trace the circle pattern eight times on each strip and cut on marked lines to make 24 center yo-yos.

7. Cut (18) 5¼" by fabric width strips multicolored floral; trace circle pattern eight times on each strip and cut on marked lines to make 144 flower yo-yos.

8. Cut eight 2¼" by fabric width strips multicolored floral for binding.

> ### Tip
>
> *If you get tired of making yo-yos when making larger versions of this quilt, alternate Flower blocks with plain blocks in the rows. This would cut the number of yo-yos needed nearly in half.*
>
> *Plain borders may be added to the larger sizes to add width and length as needed.*

9. Cut one 2½" by fabric width strip green mini-floral; subcut strip into four 2½" H squares.

Completing the Flower Blocks

1. Knot a length of quilting thread or doubled all-purpose thread; with the wrong side of a yo-yo circle facing you, begin turning a ⅛" hem to the wrong side as you sew running stitches all around close to the folded edge as shown in Figure 1. *Note: The stitches should be evenly sized and about ¼" long.*

Figure 1

2. Pull the thread to tightly gather the fabric. Smooth and flatten the circle with your fingers, pushing the hole to the center front, again referring to Figure 1; knot and clip the thread.

3. Repeat steps 1 and 2 to make a total of 144 flower yo-yos and 24 center yo-yos.

4. To complete one Flower block, fold one A square in half vertically, horizontally and diagonally, and crease to mark the centers.

5. Place a center yo-yo on the center crease, with open side up; pin to hold in place.

6. Arrange six flower yo-yos around and approximately ⅛" from the center yo-yo as shown in Figure 2; if desired, lift each yo-yo and apply a dot of fabric glue to the wrong side and put back in place. *Note: The fabric glue will hold the yo-yos in place better than pins when stitching in place.*

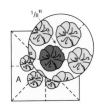

Figure 2

7. Using thread to match fabric, blindstitch around edges of each yo-yo to hold in place. *Note: Since there are no raw edges to protect, the stitches can be farther apart than usual—⅜"-long stitches will adequately hold the flower in place.*

8. Prepare a template for the leaf pattern given.

9. Trace the leaf pattern 96 times on the wrong side of the green mini-floral, leaving a ⅜" margin between shapes and marking on only one half of the fabric width. Fold the marked fabric in half with right sides together and traced shapes on top; pin the layered fabric to the fleece.

10. Stitch all around each leaf on the marked lines through all layers; cut out each leaf ⅛" from the stitched seam. Trim the tip and clip curves.

11. Cut a vertical slit through one layer only of the fabric of each leaf and turn right side out through the slit; press well.

12. Transfer the vein lines from the pattern to the right side (no slit) of four leaves using the air/water soluble pen.

13. Pin a leaf in each corner of one block with tip pointed toward the corners and about ⅝" from each side as shown in Figure 3. *Note: The centerline of each leaf should be on a diagonal crease line.*

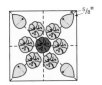

Figure 3

14. Using thread to match fabric, start machine stitching near the base of a leaf, almost up to the tip. Turn the block and start to stitch back down the line, stopping to stitch each diagonal vein as shown in Figure 4. Repeat for the remaining three leaves to complete one Flower block.

Figure 4

15. Repeat steps 4–14 to complete 24 Flower blocks.

Completing Corner Blocks

Note: Use a ¼" seam allowance for all stitching. Sew all seams with right sides together.

1. Sew an H square between two G squares as shown in Figure 5; press seams toward H.

Figure 5

House of White Birches, Berne, Indiana 46711 Clotilde.com

2. Sew an F strip to each side of the G-H unit to complete one Corner block referring to the block drawing; press seams toward F strips.

3. Repeat steps 1 and 2 to complete four Corner blocks.

Finishing the Top

1. Join two Corner blocks, five E strips and four D border rectangles to complete the top row as shown in Figure 6; press seams toward E strips. Repeat to make the bottom row.

2. Join four Flower blocks, five B strips and two D rectangles to complete a block row referring to Figure 7; press seams toward B strips. Repeat to make six block rows.

3. Join five C squares, two E strips and four B strips to make a sashing row referring to Figure 8; press seams toward B strips. Repeat to make seven sashing rows.

4. Arrange and join the rows referring to the Placement Diagram for positioning; press seams toward sashing rows.

Finishing the Quilt

1. Sandwich batting between the completed top and prepared backing piece; pin or baste layers together to hold flat.

Figure 6

2. Quilt as desired by hand or machine; remove pins or basting. Trim batting and backing even with the top.

Figure 7

3. Join the binding strips with right sides together on short ends to make one long strip; press seams open.

Figure 8

4. Press the strip in half with wrong sides together along length.

5. Sew the binding to the right side of the quilt edges, mitering corners and overlapping ends.

6. Fold binding to the back side and stitch in place.

7. Cut (28) 1½"-diameter circles from the cream mini-floral. Refer to manufacturer's instructions to cover the buttons with the fabric circles.

8. Sew one button to the center of each center yo-yo in each Flower block, sewing through all layers. Sew a button to the center of each Corner block. ❖

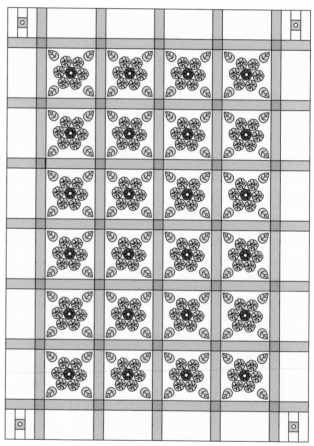

Twin-Size Yo-Yo Garden
Placement Diagram 62" x 86"

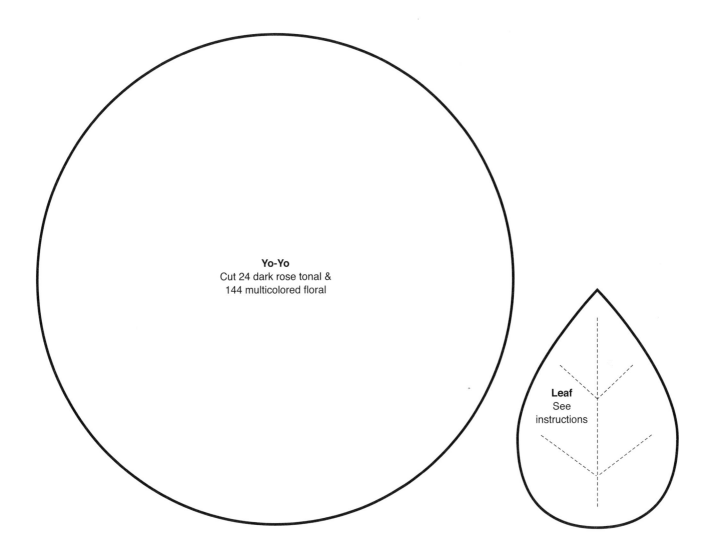

Yo-Yo
Cut 24 dark rose tonal &
144 multicolored floral

Leaf
See
instructions

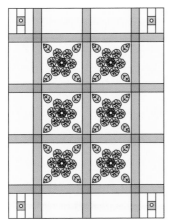

Crib-Size Yo-Yo Garden
Placement Diagram 38" x 50"

Crib-Size Yo-Yo Garden Quilt

38" x 50"
6 Flower blocks–10" x 10"
4 Corner blocks–6" x 6"
6 A squares (4 strips)
17 B sashing strips (2 strips)
12 C sashing squares (1 strip)
10 D border rectangles (with A)
14 E strips (1 strip)
8 F strips (1 strip)
8 G squares (with F)
4 H squares (1 strip)
36 flower yo-yos (5 strips)
6 center yo-yos (1 strip)
24 leaves
5 binding strips

Materials
• ⅓ yard dark rose tonal
• ⅓ yard green mini-floral
• 1 yard green/rose floral
• 1¼ yards multicolored floral
• 1½ yards cream mini-floral
• ⅓ yard thin fleece
• Batting 44" x 56"
• Backing 44" x 56"
Eliminate covered buttons if making for a baby.

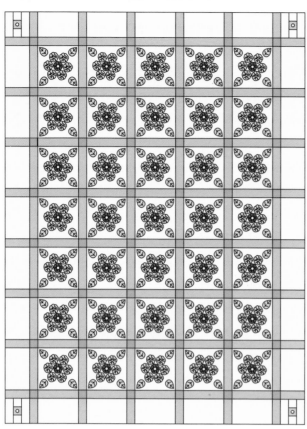

Full-Size Yo-Yo Garden
Placement Diagram 74" x 98"

Full-Size Yo-Yo Garden Quilt

74 x 98"
35 Flower blocks–10" x 10"
4 Corner blocks–6" x 6"
35 A squares (13 strips)
82 B sashing strips (6 strips)
48 C sashing squares (3 strips)
24 D border rectangles (with A)
28 E strips (2 strips)
8 F strips (1 strip)
8 G squares (with F)
4 H squares (1 strip)
210 flower yo-yos (27 strips)
35 center yo-yos (5 strips)
140 leaves
9 binding strips

Materials
- 1⅛ yards dark rose tonal
- 1¼ yards green mini-floral
- 2¼ yards green/rose floral
- 4¼ yards cream mini-floral
- 4¾ yards multicolored floral
- 1¼ yards thin fleece
- Batting 80" x 104"
- Backing 80" x 104"
- 39 covered buttons

Queen-Size Yo-Yo Garden
Placement Diagram 86" x 98"

Queen-Size Yo-Yo Garden Quilt

86" x 98"
42 Flower blocks–10" x 10"
4 Corner blocks–6" x 6"
42 A squares (15 strips)
97 B sashing strips (7 strips)
56 C sashing squares (4 strips)
26 D border rectangles (with A)
30 E strips (2 strips)
8 F strips (1 strip)
8 G squares (with F)
4 H squares (1 strip)
252 flower yo-yos (32 strips)
42 center yo-yos (6 strips)
168 leaves
10 binding strips

Materials
- 1⅓ yards dark rose tonal
- 1½ yards green mini-floral
- 2½ yards green/rose floral
- 4¾ yards cream mini-floral
- 5½ yards multicolored floral
- 1½ yards thin fleece
- Batting 92" x 104"
- Backing 92" x 104"
- 46 covered buttons

King-Size Yo-Yo Garden
Placement Diagram 98" x 110"

King-Size Yo-Yo Garden Quilt

98" x 110"
56 Flower blocks–10" x 10"
4 Corner blocks–6" x 6"
56 A squares (19 strips)
127 B sashing strips (8 strips)
72 C sashing squares (5 strips)
30 D border rectangles (with A)
34 E strips (3 strips)
8 F strips (1 strip)
8 G squares (with F)
4 H squares (1 strip)
336 flower yo-yos (42 strips)
56 center yo-yos (7 strips)
224 leaves
11 binding strips

Materials

- 1½ yards dark rose tonal
- 2 yards green mini-floral
- 3 yards green/rose floral
- 5⅞ yards cream mini-floral
- 7 yards multicolored floral
- 2 yards thin fleece
- Batting 104" x 116"
- Backing 104" x 116"
- 60 covered buttons

House of White Birches, Berne, Indiana 46711   Clotilde.com

Peppermint Twist

Design by Julie Weaver

A diagonal setting with sashing strips makes the blocks stand out in this eye-catching quilt.

Adjusting the Quilt Size

When increasing or decreasing the size of a quilt that has blocks set on point, you need to find the length of the diagonal of the block. In this case, a 10" block is 14⅛" from corner to corner. Adding sashing to the block complicates things a little. Then you need to also add the diagonal size of the sashing width. The sashing for this block is a finished width of 1". The diagonal of a 1" square is 1⅜", so for this quilt adding or decreasing by a block/sashing will mean a change of 15½".

Project Specifications
- Skill Level: Intermediate
- Quilt Size: 50¼" x 65¾"
- Block Size: 10" x 10"
- Number of Blocks: 8

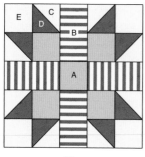

Star
10" x 10" Block
Make 6

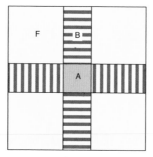

Cross
10" x 10" Block
Make 2

Materials
- ⅓ yard green tonal
- ⅝ yard cream print
- ⅞ yard cream floral
- 1 yard coral dot
- 1 yard coordinating stripe
- 1⅜ yards coral floral
- Batting 56" x 72"
- Backing 56" x 72"
- All-purpose thread to match fabrics
- Quilting thread
- Basic sewing tools and supplies

Tip

Diagonal settings result in unusual sizes for border strips. It is important to cut the large setting triangles with the grain on the long outer edge to avoid stretching on the edges of the quilt center. This is accomplished by cutting a square to the proper size and then cutting it on both diagonals to make four triangles from each square.

Cutting

1. Cut two 2½" by fabric width strips green tonal; subcut strips into (32) 2½" A squares.

2. Cut one 2" by fabric width strip green tonal; subcut strip into four 2" T squares, five 1⅞" x 1⅞" G squares and (11) 1½" x 1½" H squares. Cut each G square in half on one diagonal to make 10 G triangles.

3. Cut four 2½" by fabric width strips coordinating stripe; subcut strips into (32) 4½" B rectangles.

4. Cut three 1½" N strips coordinating stripe.

5. Cut two 1½" x 34¾" O strips coordinating stripe.

6. Cut six 2" by fabric width R/S strips coordinating stripe.

7. Cut two 2⅞" by fabric width strips cream print; subcut strips into (24) 2⅞" C squares. Cut each square in half on one diagonal to make 48 C triangles.

8. Cut two 2½" by fabric width strips cream print; subcut strips into (24) 2½" E squares.

9. Cut one 4½" by fabric width strip cream print; subcut strip into eight 4½" F squares.

10. Cut one 10½" by fabric width strip coral dot; subcut strip into (24) 1½" I strips.

11. Cut two 2⅞" by fabric width strips coral dot; subcut strips into (24) 2⅞" D squares. Cut each square in half on one diagonal to make 48 D triangles.

12. Cut six 2¼" by fabric width strips coral dot for binding.

13. Cut one 15½" by fabric width strip cream floral; subcut strip into two 15½" squares. Cut each square on both diagonals to make eight K triangles; discard 2.

14. Cut one 8" by fabric width strip cream floral; subcut strip into two 8" squares; cut each square in half on one diagonal to make four J triangles.

15. Cut two 2" x 34¾" M strips coral floral.

16. Cut three 2" by fabric width L strips coral floral.

17. Cut six 6" by fabric width P/Q strips coral floral.

Completing the Star Blocks
Note: Use a ¼" seam allowance for all stitching. Sew all seams with right sides together.

1. To complete one Star block sew C to D along the diagonals to make a C-D unit; press seam toward D. Repeat to make eight C-D units.

2. Sew E to one C-D unit as shown in Figure 1; press seam toward E. Repeat to make four C-D-E units.

Figure 1

3. Sew a C-D unit to A to make an A-C-D unit, again referring to Figure 1; repeat to make four A-C-D units.

4. Sew a C-D-E unit to an A-C-D unit to make a corner unit as shown in Figure 2; press seam in one direction. Repeat to make four corner units.

Figure 2

5. Join two corner units with B to make a row as shown in Figure 3; press seams toward B. Repeat to make two rows.

Figure 3

6. Sew A between two B rectangles to make a row; press seams toward B.

7. Join the rows referring to the block drawing to complete one Star block; press seams toward the center row.

8. Repeat steps 1–7 to complete six Star blocks.

Completing the Cross Blocks
1. To complete one Cross block, sew B between two F squares to make a B-F row; press seams toward F. Repeat to make two B-F rows.

2. Sew A between two B rectangles to make an A-B row; press seams toward A.

3. Sew the A-B row between the two B-F rows to complete one Cross block; press seams toward the B-F rows.

4. Repeat steps 1–3 to complete two Cross blocks.

Finishing the Top
1. Sew an I strip to two opposite sides of each Star block; press seams toward I strips.

2. Join three I strips with two H squares and add a G triangle to each end to make a short sashing strip as shown in Figure 4; repeat to make two short sashing strips. Press seams toward I strips.

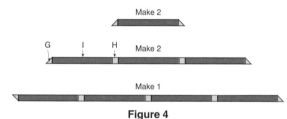

Figure 4

3. Join four I strips with three H squares and two G triangles to make a long sashing strip, again referring to Figure 4; press seams toward I strips.

4. Sew a G triangle to each end of each remaining I strip to make two end strips, again referring to Figure 4; press seams toward I strips.

5. Join two sashed Star blocks with one Cross block to make a block row; press seams toward sashed Star blocks. Repeat to make two blocks rows.

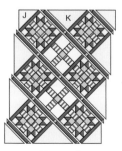

Figure 5

6. Arrange and join the sashed blocks, the block rows, sashing rows and end strips with the J and K triangles as shown in Figure 5; press seams toward sashing rows and end strips to complete the pieced center.

7. Join the L strips on short ends to make one long strip; press seams open. Subcut strip into two 47¼" L strips.

8. Sew L strips to opposite long sides and M strips to the top and bottom of the pieced center; press seams toward L and M strips.

9. Join N strips on short ends to make one long strip; press seams open. Subcut strip into two 50¼" N strips.

10. Sew N strips to opposite long sides; press seams toward N strips. Sew an H square to each end of each O strip; press seams toward O. Sew an H-O strip to the top and bottom of the pieced center; press seams toward H-O strips.

11. Join the P/Q strips on short ends to make one long strip; press seams open. Subcut strip into two 52¼" P strips and two 47¾" Q strips.

12. Sew the P strips to opposite long sides and Q strips to the top and bottom of the pieced center; press seams toward P and Q strips.

13. Repeat step 11 with R/S strips to cut two 63¼" R strips and two 47¾" S strips.

14. Sew the R strips to opposite long sides of the pieced center; press seams toward R strips.

15. Sew a T square to each end of each S strip; press seams toward S strips. Sew an S-T strip to the top and bottom of the pieced center; press seams toward S-T strips to complete the pieced top.

Finishing the Quilt

1. Sandwich batting between the completed top and prepared backing piece; pin or baste layers together to hold flat.

2. Quilt as desired by hand or machine; remove pins or basting. Trim batting and backing even with the top.

3. Join the binding strips with right sides together on short ends to make one long strip; press seams open.

4. Press the strip in half with wrong sides together along length.

5. Sew the binding to the right side of the quilt edges, mitering corners and overlapping ends.

6. Fold binding to the back side and stitch in place. ❖

Lap-Size Peppermint Twist
Placement Diagram 50¼" x 65¾"

Twin-Size Peppermint Twist
Placement Diagram 65¾" x 81¼"

Twin-Size Peppermint Twist

65¾" x 81¼"

12 Star blocks–10" x 10"

6 Cross blocks–10" x 10"

66 A squares (5 strips)

72 B rectangles (8 strips)

48 C squares (4 strips to make 96 C triangles)

48 D squares (4 strips to make 96 D triangles)

48 E squares (3 strips)

24 F squares (3 strips)

7 G squares (with T to make 14 G triangles)

21 H squares (1 strip 1½" wide)

48 I strips (2 strips)

2 J squares (1 strip to make 4 J triangles)

3 K squares (2 strips to make 12 K triangles)

6 L/M strips (2 each–62¾" L, 50¼" M)

6 N/O strips (2 each–65¾" N, 50¼" O)

7 P/Q strips (2 each–67¾" P, 63¼" Q)

7 R/S strips (2 each–78¾" R, 63¼" S)

4 T squares (1 strip)

8 binding strips

Materials

- ⅝ yard green tonal
- 1⅛ yards cream print
- 1¼ yards cream floral
- 1⅓ yards coordinating stripe
- 1⅝ yards coral dot
- 1⅞ yards coral floral
- Batting 72" x 88"
- Backing 72" x 88"

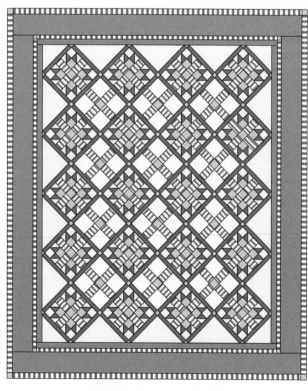

Full-Size Peppermint Twist
Placement Diagram 81¼" x 96¾"

Full-Size Peppermint Twist

81¼" x 96¾"

20 Star blocks–10" x 10"

12 Cross blocks–10" x 10"

112 A squares (7 strips)

128 B rectangles (14 strips)

80 C squares (6 strips to make 160 C triangles)

80 D squares (6 strips to make 160 D triangles)

80 E squares (5 strips)

48 F squares (6 strips)

9 G squares (with T to make 18 G triangles)

35 H squares (2 strips 1½" wide)

80 I strips (3 strips)

2 J squares (1 strip to make 4 J triangles)

4 K squares (2 strips to make 16 K triangles)

7 L/M strips (2 each–78¼" L, 65¾" M)

7 N/O strips (2 each–81¼" N, 65¾" O)

8 P/Q strips (2 each–83¼" P, 78¾" Q)

9 R/S strips (2 each–94¼" R, 78¾" S)

4 T squares (1 strip)

9 binding strips

Materials

- ¾ yard green tonal
- 1⅔ yards cream floral
- 1¾ yards cream print
- 1⅞ yards coral floral
- 2 yards coordinating stripe
- 2¼ yards coral dot
- Batting 88" x 103"
- Backing 88" x 103"

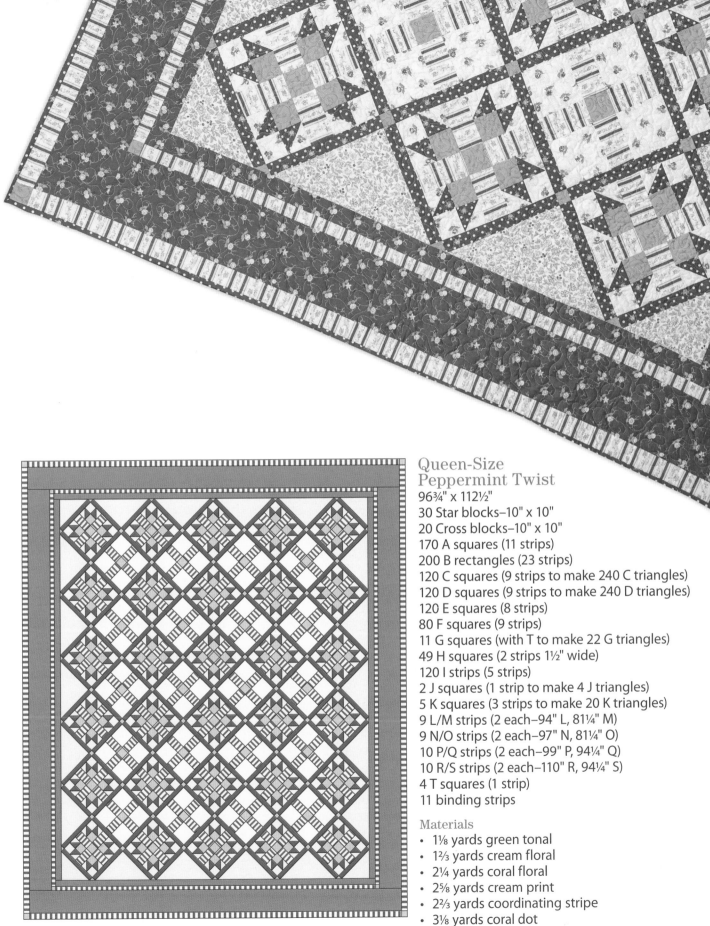

Queen-Size Peppermint Twist

96¾" x 112½"

30 Star blocks–10" x 10"
20 Cross blocks–10" x 10"
170 A squares (11 strips)
200 B rectangles (23 strips)
120 C squares (9 strips to make 240 C triangles)
120 D squares (9 strips to make 240 D triangles)
120 E squares (8 strips)
80 F squares (9 strips)
11 G squares (with T to make 22 G triangles)
49 H squares (2 strips 1½" wide)
120 I strips (5 strips)
2 J squares (1 strip to make 4 J triangles)
5 K squares (3 strips to make 20 K triangles)
9 L/M strips (2 each–94" L, 81¼" M)
9 N/O strips (2 each–97" N, 81¼" O)
10 P/Q strips (2 each–99" P, 94¼" Q)
10 R/S strips (2 each–110" R, 94¼" S)
4 T squares (1 strip)
11 binding strips

Materials

- 1⅛ yards green tonal
- 1⅔ yards cream floral
- 2¼ yards coral floral
- 2⅝ yards cream print
- 2⅔ yards coordinating stripe
- 3⅛ yards coral dot
- Batting 103" x 119"
- Backing 103" x 119"

Queen-Size Peppermint Twist
Placement Diagram 96¾" x 112½"

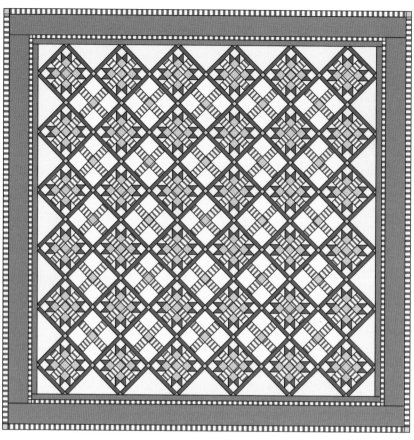

King-Size Peppermint Twist
Placement Diagram 112½" x 112½"

King-Size Peppermint Twist

112½" x 112½"
36 Star blocks–10" x 10"
25 Cross blocks–10" x 10"
205 A squares (13 strips)
244 B rectangles (28 strips)
144 C squares (11 strips to make 288 C triangles)
144 D squares (11 strips to make 288 D triangles)
144 E squares (9 strips)
100 F squares (11 strips)
12 G squares (with T to make 24 G triangles)
60 H squares (3 strips 1½" wide)
144 I strips (6 strips)
2 J squares (1 strip to make 4 J triangles)
5 K squares (3 strips to make 20 K triangles)
10 L/M strips (2 each–94" L, 97" M)
10 N/O strips (2 each–97" N, 97" O)
10 P/Q strips (2 each–99" P, 110" Q)
11 R/S strips (2 each–110" R, 110" S)
4 T squares (1 strip)
11 binding strips

Materials

- 1¼ yards green tonal
- 1⅔ yards cream floral
- 2½ yards coral floral
- 3¼ yards cream print
- 3¼ yards coordinating stripe
- 3⅝ yards coral dot
- Batting 119" x 119"
- Backing 119" x 119"

Baby Bow Tie

Design by Lisa Moore

Create a homespun look by using checked fabrics around the bunny-print octagons in this pretty little quilt.

Adjusting the Quilt Size

Although this quilt appears to be easy to stitch with its snowball blocks alternating with rectangles and squares, the number of fabrics used and the color placement make this a difficult quilt to increase or decrease in size. If you have a complex quilt like this one, whether it has a complicated design or a unique arrangement of colors, adding borders is the easiest way to make a change in the quilt size. If you need to make a big change by adding blocks, the best way to be sure everything is in the correct place is to lay out all the blocks on a flat surface, and check the placement before you begin to stitch them together. Enlarging the Placement Diagram given and adding dividing lines to the enlargement to create units on the drawing will help you place the pieces in the right combinations and color order.

Tip

The sample quilt shown was made in pastel baby-print fabrics. This coloration would work for younger children, but not for teens or adults. Substitute fabrics in different color schemes. The important thing to remember is to find three fabrics in the same color family in four different shades. The design will take on a very different appearance when made with different colors and shades of fabrics

Project Specifications
Skill Level: Intermediate
Quilt Size: 34" x 43"

Materials
- ¼ yard each blue tonal, check and bunny print
- ¼ yard each yellow tonal, check and bunny print
- ¼ yard each pink tonal, check and bunny print
- ¼ yard each green check and bunny print
- ⅝ yard green tonal
- ⅞ yard cream/blue floral
- Batting 40" x 49"
- Backing 40" x 49"
- Neutral-color all-purpose thread
- Quilting thread
- Basic sewing tools and supplies

Cutting

1. Cut one 2" by fabric width strip each blue tonal (F) and blue check (I); subcut each strip into 12 each 2" squares for F and I.

2. Cut one 2¾" by fabric width strip blue tonal; subcut strip into six 2¾" D squares and three 5" E rectangles.

3. Repeat step 2 with blue check to make six G squares and three H rectangles.

4. Cut three 5" x 5" J squares blue bunny print with motif centered. Repeat with yellow (Q), pink (X) and green (EE) bunny prints to cut three each Q, X and EE squares.

5. Repeat steps 1 and 2 with yellow tonal (M–2" and K–2¾" squares, L rectangles) and yellow check (P–2" and N–2¾" squares and O rectangles).

6. Repeat steps 1 and 2 with pink tonal (T–2" and R–2¾" squares and S rectangles) and pink check (W–2" and U–2¾" squares and V rectangles).

7. Repeat steps 1 and 2 with green tonal (AA–2" and Y–2¾" squares and Z rectangles) and green check (DD–2" and BB–2¾" squares and CC rectangles).

8. Cut four 2¼" by fabric width strips green tonal for binding.

9. Cut two 5" by fabric width strips cream/blue floral; subcut strips into six 5" A squares, (10) 2¾" B rectangles and four 2¾" x 2¾" C squares.

10. Cut two 4" x 36½" FF strips and two 4" x 34½" GG strips cream/blue floral.

Completing the Units

1. Draw a diagonal line from corner to corner on the wrong side of each F, I, M, P, T, W, DD and AA square.

2. Place an F square on one corner of C and stitch on the marked line as shown in Figure 1; trim seam to ¼" and press F to the right side to complete one C-F unit, again referring to Figure 1.

Figure 1

3. Repeat step 2 to complete one each C-W, C-M and C-DD units as shown in Figure 2.

Figure 2

4. Sew D to G to complete one D-G unit as shown in Figure 3; press seam toward G. Repeat to complete six D-G units.

Figure 3

5. Repeat step 4 to complete six each K-N, R-U and Y-BB, again referring to Figure 3; press seams toward darker fabric.

6. Sew F to two sides and I to the remaining two sides of J as in Step 2 to complete one F-I-J unit as shown in Figure 4; repeat to make three F-I-J units.

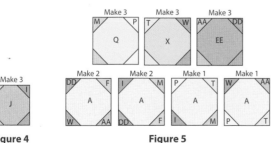

Figure 4   **Figure 5**

7. Repeat step 6 to make three each M-P-Q, T-W-X, AA-DD-EE, two each A-DD-F-W-AA, and A-DD-F-I-M and one each A-I-M-P-T and A-P-T-W-AA units as shown in Figure 5.

8. Sew I to one end and M to the opposite end of B to make a B-I-M unit as in step 2 and referring to Figure 6.

Figure 6

9. Repeat step 8 to make one B-P-T and one reversed B-P-T unit and one each B-W-AA, B-F-AA, B-W-P, B-AA-T, B-I-P, B-T-M and B-I-DD as shown in Figure 7.

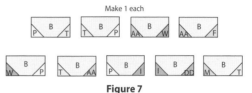

Figure 7

Completing the Quilt

1. Arrange the pieced units in rows with the CC, E, H, L, O, S, V and Z rectangles referring to Figure 8; join in rows. Join the rows as arranged to complete the pieced center.

2. Sew FF strips to opposite long sides and GG strips to the top and bottom of the pieced center; press seams toward FF and GG strips.

Finishing the Quilt

1. Sandwich batting between the completed top and prepared backing piece; pin or baste layers together to hold flat.

2. Quilt as desired by hand or machine; remove pins or basting. Trim batting and backing even with the top.

3. Join the binding strips with right sides together on short ends to make one long strip; press seams open.

4. Press the strip in half with wrong sides together along length.

5. Sew the binding to the right side of the quilt edges, mitering corners and overlapping ends.

6. Fold binding to the back side and stitch in place. ❖

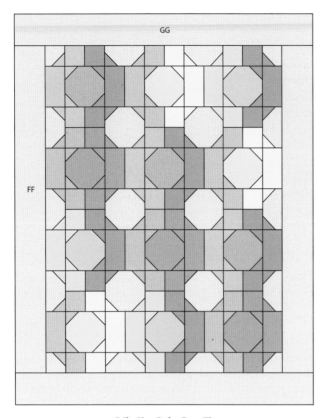

Crib-Size Baby Bow Tie
Placement Diagram 34" x 43"

Twin-Size Baby Bow Tie
Placement Diagram 72¼" x 90¼"

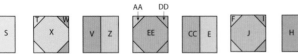

Figure 8

Twin-Size Bow Tie

72¼" x 90¼"
63 A squares (8 strips)
16 B rectangles (2 strips 2¾" wide)
1 C square (with A)
34 each D, G, K and N squares (3 strips each)
18 each E, L, S and Z rectangles (3 strips each)
68 each F, I, M and P squares (4 strips each)
16 each H, O and V rectangles (2 strips each)
16 each J, Q and X squares (2 strips each)
33 each R and U squares (3 strips each)
72 T squares (4 strips)
63 W squares (4 strips)
32 each Y and BB squares (3 strips each)
69 AA squares (4 strips)
15 CC rectangles (2 strips)
61 DD squares (3 strips)
15 EE squares (2 strips)
8 FF/GG strips (83¾" FF, 72¾" GG)
9 binding strips

Materials
- ⅜ yard each blue, yellow, green and pink bunny prints
- 1 yard each blue, yellow and pink tonals
- 1 yard each blue, yellow, green and pink checks
- 1⅝ yards green tonal
- 2¼ yards cream/blue floral
- Batting 79" x 97"
- Backing 79" x 97"

Full-Size Baby Bow Tie
Placement Diagram 81¼" x 90¼"

Full-Size Bow Tie

81¼" x 90¼"
72 A squares (9 strips)
16 B rectangles (2 strips
   2¾" wide)
1 C square (1 strip)
38 each D, G, K, N, R, U, Y
   and BB squares
   (3 strips each)
21 E rectangles (3 strips)
77 F squares (4 strips)
18 each H, O, V and CC
   rectangles (3 strips each)
76 each I, M and P squares (4
   strips each)
18 each J, Q, X and EE
   squares (3 strips each)
20 each L, S and Z
   rectangles (3 strips each)
80 each T and AA squares (4
   strips each)
72 each W and DD squares
   (4 strips each)
8 FF/GG strips (2 each–
   83¾" FF,
   81¾" GG)
9 binding strips

Materials
- ⅝ yard each blue,
  yellow, green and
  pink bunny prints
- 1 yard each green and
  pink checks
- 1⅛ yards each blue and
  yellow checks
- 1⅛ yards each blue,
  yellow and pink tonals
- 1⅔ yards green tonal
- 2½ yards cream/
  blue floral
- Batting 88" x 97"
- Backing 88" x 97"

Queen-Size Baby Bow Tie
Placement Diagram 90¼" x 99¼"

Queen-Size Bow Tie

90¼" x 99¼"
90 A squares (12 strips)
18 B rectangles (2 strips 2¾" wide)
1 C square (with B)
48 each D, G, Y and BB squares (4 strips each)
26 E rectangles (4 strips)
98 F squares (5 strips)
23 each H and CC rectangles (3 strips each)
95 I squares (5 strips)
23 each J and EE squares (3 strips each)
46 each K and N squares (4 strips each)
25 each L and Z rectangles (4 strips each)
22 each O and V rectangles (3 strips each)
93 M squares (5 strips)
92 each P and DD squares (5 strips each)
22 each Q and X squares (3 strips each)
47 each R and U squares (4 strips each)
24 S rectangles (3 strips)
97 T squares (5 strips)
89 W squares (5 strips)
101 AA squares (5 strips)
9 FF/GG strips (2 each–92¾" FF, 90¾" GG)
10 binding strips

Materials
- ⅝ yard each blue, yellow, green and pink bunny prints
- 1⅛ yards pink check
- 1¼ yards each green, blue and yellow checks
- 1¼ yards each blue, yellow and pink tonals
- 2 yards green tonal
- 3⅛ yards cream/blue floral
- Batting 97" x 106"
- Backing 97" x 106"

King-Size Baby Bow Tie
Placement Diagram 99¼" x 103¾"

King-Size Bow Tie

99¼" x 103¾"
100 A squares (13 strips)
20 B rectangles (2 strips 2¾" wide)
1 C square (with A)
54 each D and G squares (6 strips each)
31 E rectangles (4 strips)
113 each F and T squares (8 strips each)
28 each H and CC rectangles (4 strips each)
112 I squares (6 strips)
28 each J and EE squares (4 strips each)
52 each K and N squares (4 strips each)
30 each L, S and Z rectangles (4 strips each)
110 M squares (6 strips)
27 each O and V rectangles (4 strips each)
108 P squares (6 strips)
27 each Q and X squares (4 strips each)
51 each R and U squares (4 strips each)
103 W squares (5 strips)
53 each Y and BB squares (4 strips each)
115 AA squares (6 strips)
107 DD squares (6 strips)
10 FF/GG strips (2 each—97¼" FF, 99¾" GG)
10 binding strips

Materials
- ⅔ yard each blue, yellow, green and pink bunny prints
- 1⅓ yards each blue, green, pink and yellow checks
- 1⅓ yards each blue, yellow and pink tonals
- 2⅛ yards green tonal
- 3⅓ yards cream/blue floral
- Batting 106" x 110"
- Backing 106" x 110"

Stars, Stars, Stars

Design by Cate Tallman Evans

Shades of blue create diagonal trails across the top of this pretty star-design bed quilt.

Adjusting the Quilt Size

The blocks in this quilt are easy to stitch, but because there are six blocks in five different sizes, it is not easy to increase or decrease the size of this quilt. After you have determined how much larger or smaller you want the quilt to be, you need to look at both dimensions of the samples we give you. In some sizes, Block G is horizontal and in others it is vertical. To increase or decrease one of the dimensions of the quilt, you need to look at the inside rows or columns, not the outside rows or columns since they are different from the center of the quilt. If you want to add to the width, you need to add the same column to both sides to keep the design centered (except for the queen size where the design is centered top to bottom). If you want to increase the length, you can add to either end, depending on the row height that fits your measurements and fits the design (except for the queen size which is centered top to bottom). Changing the size of the border and adding more borders are, of course, easy changes to make.

Project Specifications

Skill Level: Advanced
Quilt Size: 81" x 81"
Standard Pillowcase Size: 32" x 21"
Block Sizes: 3¾" x 3¾", 5" x 3¾", 6¼" x 5" and 5" x 5"
Number of Blocks: 25, 42, 42 and 14

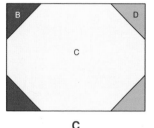

C
5" x 3¾" Block"
Make 24

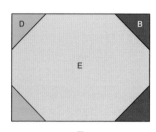

E
5" x 3¾" Block
Make 18

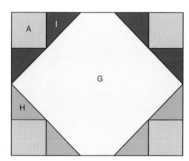

Cream G
6¼" x 5" Block
Make 24

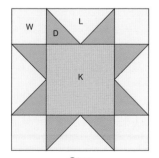

Star
5" x 5" Block
Make 14

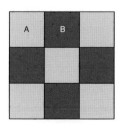

Nine-Patch
3¾" x 3¾" Block
Make 25

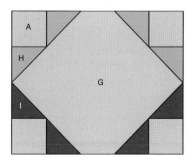

Gold G
6¼" x 5" Block
Make 18

Materials

Note: Fabric amounts based on 43" useable fabric width for this project. Fabric and cutting included to make two standard-size pillowcases.

- 1½ yards gold tonal
- 1¾ yards small floral
- 1⅞ yards light blue mottled
- 1⅞ yards dark blue mottled
- 2½ yards cream print
- 3⅜ yards large floral
- Batting 87" x 87"
- Backing 87" x 87"
- Neutral-color all-purpose thread
- Quilting thread
- Basic sewing tools and supplies

Stars, Stars, Stars Quilt

Cutting

1. Prepare templates for F and G using patterns given.

2. Cut five 5½" by fabric width strips gold tonal; subcut strips into (18) 4¼" E rectangles and G pieces as per template.

3. Cut four 3" by fabric width strips gold tonal; subcut strips into (36) 1¾" M rectangles, six 4¼" P rectangles and F pieces as per template.

4. Cut one 2⅛" by fabric width strip gold tonal; subcut strip into six 2⅛" squares; cut squares in half on one diagonal to make 12 Q triangles.

5. Cut two 1½" by fabric width strips gold tonal; subcut strips into (14) 5½" X rectangles.

6. Cut nine 1¾" by fabric width strips small floral; subcut strips into (200) 1¾" A squares.

7. Cut seven 1¾" by fabric width A strips small floral for strip sets.

8. Cut five 3" by fabric width strips small floral; subcut four strips into (50) 3" K squares and one strip into (24) 1¾" N rectangles.

9. Cut three 4¼" by fabric width strips small floral; subcut strips into (24) 4¼" R squares.

10. Cut (13) 1¾" by fabric width strips light blue mottled; subcut strips into (292) 1¾" D squares.

11. Cut six 2⅛" by fabric width light blue mottled; subcut strips into (102) 2⅛" squares. Cut each square in half on one diagonal to make 204 H triangles.

12. Cut nine 2¼" by fabric width strips light blue mottled for binding.

13. Cut (14) 1¾" by fabric width B strips dark blue mottled; set aside six strips for strip sets. Subcut remaining eight strips into (184) 1¾" B squares.

14. Cut six 2⅛" by fabric width strips dark blue mottled; subcut strips into (108) 2⅛" squares. Cut each square in half on one diagonal to make 216 I triangles.

15. Cut seven 2½" by fabric width S/T strips dark blue mottled.

16. Cut two 2½" x 42½" Y strips dark blue mottled.

17. Cut seven 5½" by fabric width strips cream print; subcut strips into (24) 4¼" C rectangles and G pieces as per template.

18. Cut two 3" by fabric width strips cream print; cut F pieces as per template.

19. Cut one 2⅛" by fabric width strip cream print; cut eight 2⅛" squares. Cut each square in half on one diagonal to make 16 J triangles.

20. Cut three 3" by fabric width strips cream print; subcut strips (48) 1¾" L rectangles and eight 4¼" O rectangles.

21. Cut seven 1¾" by fabric width strips cream print; subcut strips into (56) 1¾" W squares and (56) 3" L rectangles.

22. Cut two 5½" x 42½" AA strips cream print.

23. Cut seven 8½" by fabric width U/V strips large floral.

24. Cut two 27½" x 42½" Z pieces large floral.

Completing the C & E Blocks

1. Draw a diagonal line from corner to corner on the wrong side of each B and D square.

2. Place a B square right sides together on two adjacent corners of C as shown in Figure 1; stitch on the marked lines, trim seam allowance to ¼" and press B to the right side, again referring to Figure 1.

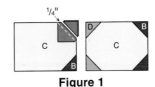

Figure 1

3. Repeat step 1 with two D squares on the remaining corners of C to complete one C block, again referring to Figure 1.

4. Repeat steps 1 and 2 to complete 24 C blocks.

5. Repeat steps 1 and 2 with E to complete 18 E blocks referring to the block drawing for positioning of B and D.

Completing the Nine-Patch Blocks

1. Cut one B strip and two A strips in half to make two 21" B strips and four 21" A strips.

2. Sew a B strip between two A strips with right sides together along the length; press seams toward B. Repeat to make two A-B-A strip sets. Repeat with half-strips to make one half-strip set.

3. Subcut the A-B-A strip sets into (50) 1¾" A-B-A units as shown in Figure 2.

Figure 2

4. Sew an A strip between two B strips with right sides together along the length to make one strip set; press seams toward B. Repeat with half strips to make one half-strip set.

5. Subcut the B-A-B strip sets into (25) 1¾" B-A-B units, again referring to Figure 2.

6. To complete one Nine-Patch block, sew a B-A-B unit between two A-B-A units referring to the block drawing; press seams in one direction. Repeat to make 25 Nine-Patch blocks.

Completing the G Blocks

1. Sew H to two adjacent sides of an A square as shown in Figure 3; press seams toward H. Repeat to make 96 A-H units. Set aside 12 A-H units for setting units.

A-H Unit   A-I Unit
Make 96   Make 100

Figure 3

2. Repeat step 1 with A and I to complete 100 A-I units, again referring to Figure 3; press seams toward I. Set aside 16 A-I units for setting units.

3. To complete one Gold G block, sew an A-H and A-I unit to one end of a gold G as shown in Figure

4; press seams toward G. Repeat on the opposite end of G to complete one block, again referring to Figure 4. Repeat to make 18 Gold G blocks.

Figure 4

4. Repeat step 3 with cream G pieces to make 24 Cream G blocks referring to the block drawing for positioning of units.

Completing the Setting Units

1. Sew I to J and add A to make a corner unit as shown in Figure 5; press seams toward I and then toward A. Repeat to make two corner units and two reverse corner units, again referring to Figure 5.

Corner Unit   Reverse Corner Unit
Make 2   Make 2

Figure 5

2. Sew an A-I unit to each angled end of a cream F piece to complete a cream F unit as shown in Figure 6; press seams toward F. Repeat to make eight cream F units.

Cream F Unit   Gold F Unit
Make 8   Make 6

Figure 6

3. Repeat step 2 with A-H units and gold F pieces to complete six gold F units, again referring to Figure 6.

4. Place D on L and stitch on the marked line as shown in Figure 7; trim seam to ¼" and press D to the right side.

¼"   B-D-L   Reverse B-D-L
Make 24   Make 24

Figure 7

5. Repeat with B on the opposite end of L to complete one B-D-L unit, again referring to Figure 7. Repeat to complete 24 B-D-L units.

6. Repeat steps 4 and 5 to complete 24 reverse B-D-L units, again referring to Figure 7.

7. Add N to six each B-D-L and reverse B-D-L units to complete six each N and reverse N units as shown in Figure 8; press seams toward N.

Reverse
N Unit   N Unit
Make 6   Make 6

Figure 8

8. Sew B and D to M as in steps 4 and 5 to complete 18 each B-D-M and reverse B-D-M units as shown in Figure 9.

Reverse
Make 18 Make 18

Figure 9

9. Join one each B-D-L and B-D-M unit with K to complete a K unit as shown in Figure 10; press seams toward K. Repeat to make 18 K units and 18 reverse K units, again referring to Figure 10.

Reverse
K Unit   K Unit
Make 18 Make 18

Figure 10

10. Referring to Figure 11, place B on each end of O and stitch on the marked line; trim seam to ¼" and press B to the right side to complete one O unit. Repeat to complete eight O units.

Make 8   Make 6

Figure 11

11. Repeat step 10 with D and P to complete six P units, again referring to Figure 11.

12. Sew I to J and H to Q along the diagonals; repeat to make 12 units each.

13. Sew an I-J and H-Q unit to N as shown in Figure 12 to complete a side unit; press seams toward N. Repeat to complete six side units.

Reverse
Side Unit Side Unit
Make 6   Make 6

Figure 12

14. Repeat step 13 to complete six reversed side units, again referring to Figure 12.

Completing the Quilt

1. Arrange and join one corner unit, one reverse corner unit, four cream F units, three gold F units and three each N and reverse N units to make the top row as shown in Figure 13; press seams toward the F units. Repeat to make the bottom row.

Make 2

Figure 13

2. Join two O units, three R squares, four Nine-Patch blocks, and six C blocks to make an X row as shown in Figure 14; press seams away from Nine-Patch blocks and toward R. Repeat to make four X rows.

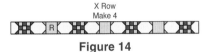

X Row
Make 4

Figure 14

3. Arrange and join one each side and reverse side units with three Gold G and four Cream G blocks and three each K and reverse K units to complete one Y row as shown in Figure 15; press seams toward K and side units. Repeat to make six Y rows.

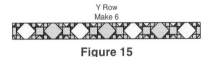

Y Row
Make 6

Figure 15

4. Arrange and join two P units with four R squares, three Nine-Patch blocks and six E blocks to complete a Z row as shown in Figure 16; press seams toward R and away from Nine-Patch blocks. Repeat to make three Z rows.

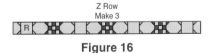

Z Row
Make 3

Figure 16

5. Arrange and join the X, Y and Z rows with the top and bottom rows to complete the pieced center referring to the Placement Diagram for positioning of rows; press seams in one direction.

6. Join the S/T strips with right sides together on short ends to make one long strip; press seams open. Subcut strip into two 61¾" S strips and two 65¾" T strips.

7. Sew the S strips to opposite sides and T strips to the top and bottom of the pieced center; press seams toward S and T strips.

8. Join the U/V strips with right sides together on short ends to make one long strip; press seams open. Subcut strip into two 65¾" U strips and two 81½" V strips.

9. Sew the U strips to opposite sides and V strips to the top and bottom of the pieced center to complete the pieced top; press seams toward the U and V strips.

Finishing the Quilt

1. Sandwich batting between the completed top and prepared backing piece; pin or baste layers together to hold flat.

2. Quilt as desired by hand or machine; remove pins or basting. Trim batting and backing even with the top.

3. Join the binding strips with right sides together on short ends to make one long strip; press seams open.

4. Press the strip in half with wrong sides together along length.

5. Sew the binding to the right side of the quilt edges, mitering corners and overlapping ends.

6. Fold binding to the back side and stitch in place to finish.

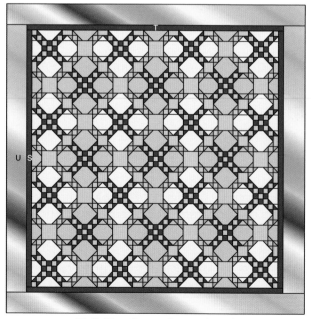

Full-Size Stars, Stars, Stars
Placement Diagram
81" x 81"

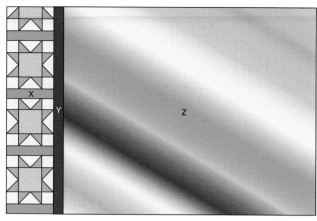

Stars, Stars, Stars Pillowcase
Placement Diagram
32" x 21"

Stars, Stars, Stars Pillowcases
Completing the Blocks

1. Referring to Figure 17, place a D square right sides together on one end of L and stitch on the marked line; trim seam to ¼" and press D to the right side.

Figure 17

2. Repeat step 1 on the remaining end of L to complete a D-L unit as shown in Figure 18. Repeat to make 56 D-L units.

Figure 18

3. To complete one Star block, sew a D-L unit to opposite sides of K to complete the center row as shown in Figure 19; press seams toward K.

Figure 19

4. Sew W to each end of two D-L units to complete two side units referring to Figure 20; press seams toward W.

Figure 20

5. Sew a side unit to opposite sides of the center row as shown in Figure 21 to complete one Star block; press seams toward the center row.

Figure 21

6. Repeat steps 3–5 to complete 14 Star blocks.

Completing the Pillowcase

1. Join seven Star blocks with seven X rectangles to make a block strip as shown in Figure 22; press seams toward X. Repeat to make two block strips.

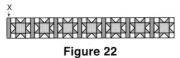

Figure 22

2. Press under ¼" on one long edge of each AA strip to hem.

3. Sew an AA strip right sides together along the length of each block strip; press seams toward AA strips.

4. Fold each Y strip with wrong sides together along the length; press.

5. Match the raw edges of each folded Y strip with one 42½" raw edge of Z; baste to hold. Repeat to make two Y-Z units.

6. Match the 42½" raw edge of each AA/block strip to each Y-Z unit and stitch; press seam toward the AA/block strips.

7. Fold each Y-Z-AA/block unit in half with right sides together, matching seams as shown in Figure 23; stitch together at bottom and side edges. Zigzag-stitch or serge seam allowance to finish. Turn right side out; press seam flat.

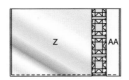

Figure 23

8. Fold the AA piece inside to cover the Y-Z-AA/block seam as shown in Figure 24; press.

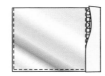

Figure 24

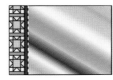

Figure 25

9. Stitch AA in place in the ditch of the seam from the right side as shown in Figure 25 to finish the pillowcases. ❖

G
Cut 18 gold tonal & 24 cream print

Crib-Size Stars, Stars, Stars
Placement Diagram
35¼" x 40¼"

Crib-Size Stars, Stars, Stars
35¼" x 40¼"

5 Nine-Patch blocks–3¾" x 3¾"
4 C blocks–5" x 3¾"
2 E blocks–5" x 3¾"
4 Cream G blocks–6¼" x 5"
2 Gold G blocks–6¼" x 5"
24 A squares (1 strip)
3 A strips for strip sets
28 B squares (2 strips)
3 B strips for strip sets
4 C rectangles (1 strip)
24 D squares (1 strip)
2 E rectangles (1 strip)
0 F cream pieces
0 F gold pieces
4 G cream pieces (with E)
2 G gold pieces (1 strip)
14 H squares (1 strip to make 28 H triangles)
14 I squares (1 strip to make 28 I triangles)
2 J squares (1 strip to make 4 J triangles)
4 K squares (1 strip)
4 L rectangles (with E)
4 M rectangles (with P)
4 N rectangles (with K)

4 O rectangles (1 strip)
2 P rectangles (1 strip)
2 Q squares (1 strip to make 4 Q triangles)
4 R squares (1 strip)
4 S/T strips (26¾" S, 25¾" T)
4 U/V strips (5" wide, 30¾" U, 35¾" V)
0 W squares
0 X rectangles
0 Y strips
0 Z pieces
0 AA strips
4 binding strips

Materials
Note: Fabric amounts based on 43" useable fabric width for this project. No yardage is included to make a pillowcase to match the crib-size quilt.

- ½ yard gold tonal
- ½ yard cream print
- ⅝ yard light blue mottled
- ⅝ yard small floral
- ¾ yard large floral
- ⅞ yard dark blue mottled
- Batting 42" x 47"
- Backing 42" x 47"

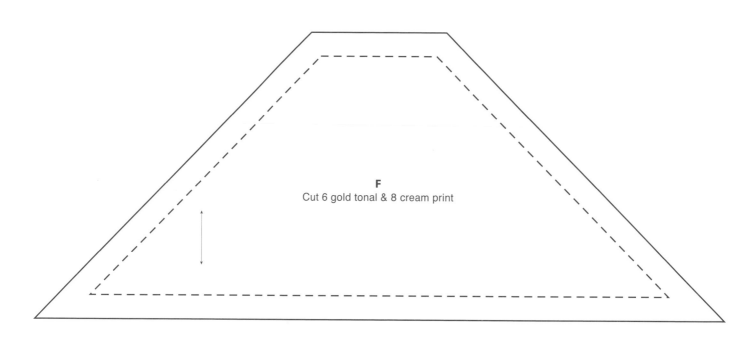

F
Cut 6 gold tonal & 8 cream print

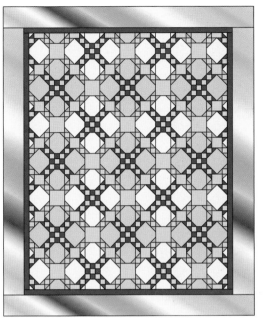

Twin-Size Stars, Stars, Stars
Placement Diagram
68¾" x 81¼"

Twin-Size Stars, Stars, Stars

68¾" x 81¼"
17 Nine-Patch blocks–3¾" x 3¾"
12 C blocks–5" x 3¾"
18 E blocks–5" x 3¾"
24 Cream G blocks–6¼" x 5"
18 Gold G blocks–6¼" x 5"
1 Star block–3¾" x 3¾" (pillowcase)
168 A squares (7 strips)
5 A strips for strip sets
140 B squares (6 strips)
4 B strips for strip sets
12 C rectangles (2 strips)
200 D squares (9 strips)
18 E rectangles (2 strips)
0 F cream pieces
0 F gold pieces
24 G cream pieces (4 strips)
18 G gold pieces (3 strips)
90 H squares (5 strips to make 180 H triangles)
90 I squares (5 strips to make 180 I triangles)
6 J squares (1 strip to make 12 J triangles)
43 K squares (4 strips)
64 L rectangles (3 strips 3" wide)
36 M rectangles (2 strips 3" wide)
12 N rectangles (1 strip)
4 O rectangles (1 strip)
6 P rectangles (1 strip)
6 Q squares (1 strip to make 12 Q triangles)

18 R squares (2 strips)
6 S/T strips (61¾" S, 53¼" T)
7 U/V strips (65¾" U, 69¼" V)
28 W squares (2 strips)
7 X rectangles (2 strips)
1 Y strip
1 Z piece
1 AA strip
8 binding strips

Materials

Note: *Fabric amounts based on 43" useable fabric width for this project. Fabrics and cutting included to make one 32" x 21" pillowcase.*

- 1¼ yards small floral
- 1⅜ yards gold tonal
- 1½ yards dark blue mottled
- 1½ yards light blue mottled
- 2 yards cream print
- 2⅝ yards large floral
- Batting 77" x 90"
- Backing 77" x 90"

Queen-Size Stars, Stars, Stars
Placement Diagram
92½" x 98¾"

Queen-Size Stars, Stars, Stars
92½" x 98¾"
36 Nine-Patch blocks–3¾" x 3¾"
32 C blocks–5" x 3¾"
32 E blocks–5" x 3¾"
40 Cream G blocks–6¼" x 5"
32 Gold G blocks–6¼" x 5"
14 Star blocks–3¾" x 3¾" (pillowcases)
308 A squares (13 strips)
8 A strips for strip sets (3 A-B-A, 2 B-A-B sets)
280 B squares (12 strips)
7 B strips for strip sets
32 C rectangles (4 strips)
392 D squares (17 strips)
32 E rectangles (4 strips)
5 F cream rectangles (1 strip)
4 F gold rectangles (1 strip)
40 G cream rectangles (7 strips)
32 G gold rectangles (6 strips)
160 H squares (9 strips to make 320 H triangles)
163 I squares (9 strips to make 326 I triangles)
9 J squares (1 strip to make 18 J triangles)
78 K squares (6 strips)
128 L rectangles (6 strips)
64 M rectangles (3 strips)
24 N rectangles (1 strip)

8 O rectangles (1 strip)
8 P rectangles (1 strip)
8 Q squares (1 strip to make 16 Q triangles)
36 R squares (4 strips)
8 S/T strips (79¼" S, 77" T)
9 U/V strips (83¼" U, 93" V)
56 W squares (3 strips)
14 X rectangles (2 strips)
2 Y strips
2 Z pieces
2 AA strips
10 binding strips

Materials
Note: *Fabric amounts based on 43" useable fabric
width for this project. Fabric and cutting is included to
make two 32" x 21" pillowcases.*

- 2¼ yards gold tonal
- 2¼ yards small floral
- 2¼ yards light blue mottled
- 2½ yards dark blue mottled
- 3⅛ yards cream print
- 4 yards large floral
- Batting 101" x 107"
- Backing 101" x 107"

King-Size Stars, Stars, Stars
Placement Diagram
98¾" x 110"

King-Size Stars, Stars, Stars

98¾" x 110"
45 Nine-Patch blocks–3¾" x 3¾"
40 C blocks–5" x 3¾"
40 E blocks–5" x 3¾"
50 Cream G blocks–6¼" x 5"
40 Gold G blocks–6¼" x 5"
14 Star blocks–3¾" x 3¾" (pillowcases)
380 A squares (16 strips)
10 A strips for strip sets
356 B squares (15 strips)
8 B strips for strip sets
40 C rectangles (5 strips)
460 D squares (20 strips)
40 E rectangles (5 strips)
5 F cream pieces (1 strip)
4 F gold pieces (1 strip)
50 G cream pieces (9 strips)
40 G gold pieces (7 strips)
198 H squares (10 strips to make 396 H triangles)
201 I squares (11 strips to make 402 I triangles)
11 J squares (1 strip to make 22 J triangles)
94 K squares (7 strips)
144 L rectangles (6 strips 3" wide)
80 M rectangles (4 strips 3" wide)
28 N rectangles (2 strips)

10 O rectangles (2 strips)
10 P rectangles (2 strips)
10 Q squares (1 strips to make 20 Q triangles)
45 R squares (5 strips)
9 S/T strips (90½" S, 83¼" T)
10 U/V strips (94½" U, 99¼" V)
56 W squares (3 strips)
14 X rectangles (2 strips)
2 Y strips
2 Z pieces (29½" x 42½")
2 AA strips
11 binding strips

Materials

Note: *Fabric amounts based on 43" useable fabric width for this project. Fabric and cutting is included to make two 40" x 21" king pillowcases.*

- 2¾ yards gold tonal
- 2¾ yards small floral
- 2¾ yards light blue mottled
- 2¾ yards dark blue mottled
- 3¼ yards cream print
- 4¼ yards large floral
- Batting 107" x 118"
- Backing 107" x 118"

Metric Conversion Charts

Metric Conversions

Canada/U.S. Measurement		Multiplied by		Metric Measurement
yards	x	.9144	=	metres (m)
yards	x	91.44	=	centimetres (cm)
inches	x	2.54	=	centimetres (cm)
inches	x	25.40	=	millimetres (mm)
inches	x	.0254	=	metres (m)

Canada/U.S. Measurement		Multiplied by		Metric Measurement
centimetres	x	.3937	=	inches
metres	x	1.0936	=	yards

Standard Equivalents

Canada/U.S. Measurement		Metric Measurement		
⅛ inch	=	3.20 mm	=	0.32 cm
¼ inch	=	6.35 mm	=	0.635 cm
⅜ inch	=	9.50 mm	=	0.95 cm
½ inch	=	12.70 mm	=	1.27 cm
⅝ inch	=	15.90 mm	=	1.59 cm
¾ inch	=	19.10 mm	=	1.91 cm
⅞ inch	=	22.20 mm	=	2.22 cm
1 inch	=	25.40 mm	=	2.54 cm
⅛ yard	=	11.43 cm	=	0.11 m
¼ yard	=	22.86 cm	=	0.23 m
⅜ yard	=	34.29 cm	=	0.34 m
½ yard	=	45.72 cm	=	0.46 m
⅝ yard	=	57.15 cm	=	0.57 m
¾ yard	=	68.58 cm	=	0.69 m
⅞ yard	=	80.00 cm	=	0.80 m
1 yard	=	91.44 cm	=	0.91 m
1⅛ yards	=	102.87 cm	=	1.03 m
1¼ yards	=	114.30 cm	=	1.14 m

Canada/U.S. Measurement		Metric Measurement		
1⅜ yards	=	125.73 cm	=	1.26 m
1½ yards	=	137.16 cm	=	1.37 m
1⅝ yards	=	148.59 cm	=	1.49 m
1¾ yards	=	160.02 cm	=	1.60 m
1⅞ yards	=	171.44 cm	=	1.71 m
2 yards	=	182.88 cm	=	1.83 m
2⅛ yards	=	194.31 cm	=	1.94 m
2¼ yards	=	205.74 cm	=	2.06 m
2⅜ yards	=	217.17 cm	=	2.17 m
2½ yards	=	228.60 cm	=	2.29 m
2⅝ yards	=	240.03 cm	=	2.40 m
2¾ yards	=	251.46 cm	=	2.51 m
2⅞ yards	=	262.88 cm	=	2.63 m
3 yards	=	274.32 cm	=	2.74 m
3⅛ yards	=	285.75 cm	=	2.86 m
3¼ yards	=	297.18 cm	=	2.97 m
3⅜ yards	=	308.61 cm	=	3.09 m
3½ yards	=	320.04 cm	=	3.20 m
3⅝ yards	=	331.47 cm	=	3.31 m
3¾ yards	=	342.90 cm	=	3.43 m
3⅞ yards	=	354.32 cm	=	3.54 m
4 yards	=	365.76 cm	=	3.66 m
4⅛ yards	=	377.19 cm	=	3.77 m
4¼ yards	=	388.62 cm	=	3.89 m
4⅜ yards	=	400.05 cm	=	4.00 m
4½ yards	=	411.48 cm	=	4.11 m
4⅝ yards	=	422.91 cm	=	4.23 m
4¾ yards	=	434.34 cm	=	4.34 m
4⅞ yards	=	445.76 cm	=	4.46 m
5 yards	=	457.20 cm	=	4.57 m

E-mail: Customer_Service@whitebirches.com

HOUSE of
WHITE
BIRCHES
PUBLISHERS
SINCE 1947

Bed Quilts Just Your Size is published by DRG, 306 East Parr Road, Berne, IN 46711, telephone (260) 589-4000. Printed in USA. Copyright © 2010 DRG. All rights reserved. This publication may not be reproduced in part or in whole without written permission from the publisher.

RETAIL STORES: If you would like to carry this pattern book or any other DRG publications, call the Wholesale Department at Annie's Attic to set up a direct account: (903) 636-4303. Also, request a complete listing of publications available from DRG.

Every effort has been made to ensure that the instructions in this pattern book are complete and accurate. We cannot, however, take responsibility for human error, typographical mistakes or variations in individual work.

STAFF

Editors: Jeanne Stauffer, Sandra L. Hatch
Assistant Editor: Erika Mann
Technical Artist: Connie Rand
Copy Supervisor: Michelle Beck
Copy Editors: Angie Buckles, Sue Harvey, Amanda Ladig
Graphic Arts Supervisor: Ronda Bechinski

Graphic Artists: Pam Gregory, Erin Augsburger
Art Director: Brad Snow
Assistant Art Director: Nick Pierce
Photography Supervisor: Tammy Christian
Photography: Matthew Owen
Photo Stylist: Tammy Steiner

ISBN: 978-1-59217-279-5
2 3 4 5 6 7 8 9

Photo Index

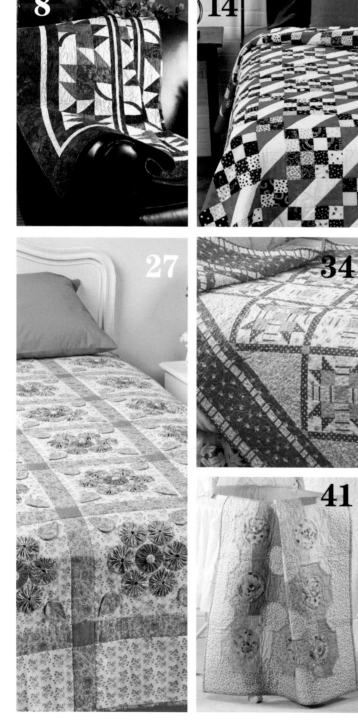

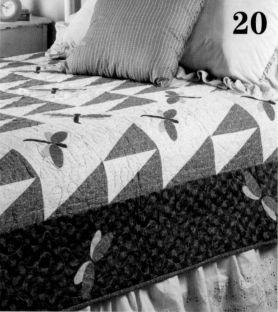